OTHER RANDOM HOUSE LAW MANUALS

Using a Lawyer
. . . And What to Do If Things Go Wrong
A Step-by-Step Guide

Small Claims Court
Making Your Way Through the System
A Step-by-Step Guide

Probate
How to Settle an Estate
A Step-by-Step Guide

REAL ESTATE
The Legal Side to Buying
a House, Condo, or Co-op
A STEP-BY-STEP GUIDE

A RANDOM HOUSE PRACTICAL LAW MANUAL

REAL ESTATE

The Legal Side to Buying a House, Condo, or Co-op

A STEP-BY-STEP GUIDE

GEORGE MILKO
in Association with HALT

RANDOM HOUSE NEW YORK

This work was originally published in different form by HALT,
An Organization of Americans for Legal Reform, in 1980. A
second edition of this work was published by HALT in 1986.

HALT is a national, non-profit, non-partisan, public-interest
group with more than 150,000 members. Based in Washington,
D.C., its goals are to enable people to handle their legal affairs
simply, affordably, and equitably. HALT's education and advo-
cacy programs strive to improve the quality, reduce the costs
and increase the accessibility of the civil justice system. Its
activities are funded by member's contributions.

Contributing authors: Chip Greenwood, Paul Hasse, and Daniel Lewolt.

Library of Congress Cataloging-in-Publication Data

Milko, George.
    Real estate: the legal side to buying a house, condo, or
co-op: a step-by-step guide/by George Milko in association
with HALT.
        p.   cm.—(A Random House practical law manual)
    Rewritten, expanded, and updated version of: Real es-
tate/Daniel Lewolt. 2nd ed. Washington, D.C.: Halt, 1986.
    Includes bibliographical references.
    ISBN 0-679-72980-1
    1. Vendors and purchasers—United States—Popular
works. 2. House buying—United States. I. Lewolt Daniel.
Real estate. II. HALT, Inc. III. Title. IV. Series.
    KF665.Z9L49   1990
    346.7304'363—dc20   90-8145
    [347.3064363]   CIP

Book design by Charlotte Staub
Manufactured in the United States of America
Revised Edition

Contents

INTRODUCTION

If you can afford it, you can buy a house, co-op or condominium* simply by sitting back and hiring professionals to make all the arrangements for you. You can find a professional for each step of the way and never do more than look at the houses they find for you, make your choice, then sign the papers they thrust in front of you. In fact, that is exactly the extent to which most people participate in the purchase of their home—they sign where and when they are told, relying blindly on the professionals.

We have prepared this book because we believe there is a better way to manage the purchase of a home. This is probably one of the most expensive purchases you will ever make. You will be served best if as much of the mystery as possible is removed from the process and if you play an active role in the decision making.

This book is intended for prospective home buyers who want to work with real estate professionals in an informed way. It introduces the professionals involved in the selling and buying of homes, describes the role of each and tells you whose interests correspond to yours and whose are opposed. The more informed you are, the better you can

---

*Throughout this manual, the terms "house," "home" and "unit" are used interchangeably. All denote the same thing for the purposes of the buyer—the residence being bought, whether it be a condo, a co-op, a single-family house or a town house.

participate in the discussions that go on among brokers, appraisers, lenders and all the others involved.

Although this book is written from a home buyer's point of view, those selling their homes will also find it useful. From whichever side you approach the process, the players and their roles in the process remain the same. It pays to be as well informed about them as possible.

HOW TO USE THIS BOOK

To get the greatest benefit from this book, especially if you are buying your first home, read the full text first and look for other resources as well. Then refer back to the book at each stage of the process and follow the specific suggestions for where you are in the process.

A WORD ABOUT TERMS

Insider knowledge of the real estate profession is communicated through many industry "terms of art," shorthand language that, like all legalese, can be needlessly complex. In many cases, the terms can be replaced with common words without loss of meaning. This book tries to use both the common, plain-language terms and the terms of art you will need to understand. When a term of art is used, it is in italics and explained in plain language. Still other terms are defined in the glossary (Appendix III). The more familiar you become with these industry terms and their meaning, the more confidently you will participate in the negotiations and make the necessary decisions.

REAL ESTATE
The Legal Side to Buying
a House, Condo, or Co-op

A STEP-BY-STEP GUIDE

CHAPTER 1

SOME GROUND RULES

Real estate consists of land and buildings. This includes everything that is naturally a part of the land, such as minerals, and everything that is more or less permanently attached to the land, such as swimming pools and fences.

Residential real estate comes in three basic forms. Single-family homes are what most people think of when they think of home buying. Condominiums and cooperatives are two alternative forms of homeownership. They are discussed in Chapter 2. All other designations—town house, apartment, unit, duplex—are merely names for one of the three kinds of homeownership.

To acquire real estate, people exchange money or something else of value. To represent and act as a record of the exchange, people draft a *contract.* Once real property is exchanged, the seller *(grantor)* gives the buyer *(grantee)* a *deed,* which is the statement filed as the record of ownership.

THE DEED

The formal representation of ownership you receive when you purchase real estate is the *deed.* It is a written instrument that states who you are, what you own and from whom you received it. It includes a specific description of the property involved and a statement that the named seller is transferring his or her interest in the land to the named buyer. It is filed as a public record, available for anyone to see.

FORMS OF PROPERTY OWNERSHIP

Whether you have a right to all or only a part of the real estate you own depends on how the deal was structured, what portion you were granted in the exchange and whether you own it alone or in partnership with someone else.

Property ownership can be in any of several different forms. The most common—and most complete—interest you can own in real estate is called the *fee simple,* or absolute ownership. When you own a fee simple interest, you own the real estate itself, everything below it (*mineral rights*) and everything above it (*air rights*). In most states, unless the document of the transfer of real estate specifies otherwise, it is assumed that the ownership being transferred is a fee simple.

Less common forms of ownership or interest in real estate include *fee tail* and *life estate.* These forms involve less than total and absolute ownership and control. The terms are derived from property law of centuries ago but are still used today in some states. More likely than not, unless you inherit land or are involved in an unusual transfer, you will be purchasing or selling a fee simple and will not need to concern yourself with these other terms. However, if you do come across them, read a textbook on property law and study their meaning carefully before you act. They are defined in the glossary (Appendix III).

You can own fee simple property alone or with someone else. If you do share ownership with one or more persons, it can be structured in any of several different ways. The way you choose will have important resale and inheritance implications.

Tenancy in Common

When two or more people share ownership of real estate, they are said to have a *tenancy in common.* Each co-owner owns a designated percentage of the property and can do as he or she pleases with it. The co-owners can sell their portions separately or leave their portions in their wills to whomever they wish. When a co-owner dies, that co-owner's interest in the property passes to the co-owner's heir, who becomes a co-owner with the surviving original owner or owners.

Joint Tenancy

Joint tenancy is also ownership of a piece of property by two or more people. However, in a joint tenancy, the co-owners can be thought of as one person. Both of them own the full 100% of the real estate. No single owner can choose to sell or dispose of any or all of the property without the agreement of the other(s). Also, the property cannot be left in a will. When a co-owner dies, the remaining co-owners assume control of the property on their own, removing any requirement of probate.

Tenancy by the Entirety

Only married couples can own property under a *tenancy by the entirety.* As in a joint tenancy, each spouse has a "right of survivorship" that enables either of them to assume total ownership when the other dies. Again, one major benefit of this form of ownership is that, when one spouse dies, the transfer of ownership is usually not subject to probate.

Community Property

Community property is recognized by the property laws of eight states: Arizona, California, Idaho, Louisiana, Nevada, New Mexico, Texas and Washington. In these states, all property owned by a married couple is considered community property. This includes all property acquired during marriage that was not a gift or inheritance to one spouse or specifically kept separate. The earnings of both spouses and any property derived from those earnings are both considered community property. In some states, income earned by separate property (e.g., rental housing owned by one spouse) is also community property.

In the eight community property states, each spouse owns half interest in all the marriage's community property. Unlike joint ownership, community property does not include any rights of survivorship. When one spouse dies, the survivor owns only his or her share of the community property (in most cases, half of all the earnings and property acquired by both spouses during the marriage).

The share owned by the spouse who has died can be transferred by his or her will, or by the state if there is no will. The deceased spouse's share of the community property usually must be probated, although this varies from state to state. Also, half of the community property owned by the spouse who died will be included in calculating estate or inheritance taxes.

Commercial Property

In real estate transactions that involve commercial property held for income or tax shelter purposes, many people choose other, more complex title-holding devices: corporations, partnerships, land trusts and real estate investment trusts (called REITs). Free information regarding these can be obtained from the trust department of most local banks or savings and loans. Because they are beyond the scope of the average home buyer's interests, they are not discussed in this book.

LOCAL CUSTOM

Even though the sale and purchase of real estate is a highly regulated field, much about the process depends on local custom that has evolved over the years among area professionals. Don't be surprised to hear things like "the buyer usually handles that" or "the buyer and seller usually split that fee." Many of these customs have to do with closing costs, but some have to do with which side is responsible for performing or arranging for a certain task, such as an inspection, to be performed. If you have a buyer's broker, look to him or her for advice. If not, you may have to rely on the seller's broker to tell you what local custom dictates or ask friends and neighbors who have bought homes in the area.

CHAPTER 2

CONDOS AND CO-OPS

Two forms of homeownership have become increasingly popular—condominiums and cooperatives. Both represent strategies for pooling home-purchasing power. They evolved in response to changing life-styles and shifting conditions in the real estate marketplace.

Ever since condominiums became popular, they have represented a growing portion of the nation's "housing starts." (Housing starts are government calculations of the number of new houses that enter the real estate market each month.) Like cooperatives, "condos" are attractive because they often enable you to own property without having to care for a yard or tend to other outdoor maintenance. They also afford potential savings on utilities.

The way you buy a condominium or cooperative differs significantly from the way you buy a traditional family house. If you are shopping for either a condominium or cooperative, you may want to supplement this book with additional materials that are specific to the subject. This book can be used for the purchase of condos and co-ops, and it points out differences between these and standard detached homes. You will also want to shop for a broker who specializes in these markets.

CONDOMINIUMS

The term *condominium,* or condo, describes a kind of ownership, not a kind of building. It is a form of ownership in which the owners of more than one home share the ownership, use and responsibility for certain common facilities. The individual owners control their own homes, or *units,* and pay a fee to have the common areas maintained. The common areas may include hallways, lobbies, parking lots and garages, recreational facilities and all of the other parts of the development not defined as a unit, including the roof.

The purchaser of a condominium unit receives a deed that gives *exclusive* ownership of the particular unit and *partial* interest in the common elements associated with the business or community in which the unit is located.

Each unit owner is automatically a member of the condominium association, the organization that operates the community as a business enterprise and insures compliance with the association's bylaws. The association elects a board of directors to run the condominium and to collect fees from the unit owners to maintain the common areas and to pay insurance and other expenses, such as utilities, that aren't paid individually.

The condominium fee may vary from building to building and from unit to unit, depending on the size and value of the unit and how the board of directors decides to structure the fees. The size of this fee should be considered before buying a unit, because it is paid in addition to the mortgage a buyer must pay. Be aware, too, that condominium fees have been known to rise steeply after the purchase. Study the terms of condo membership carefully or you may find yourself with a mortgage you planned on and provided for but a condo fee that far exceeds your expectations or ability to pay.

Condo living is available in a variety of styles: communities of single-family houses, attached town houses, apartment units in either high-rise or low-rise buildings, and garden apartments. There are condo communities for the elderly and for "singles." There are parking garage condos and commercial condos. Residential condo units can be mixed in the same building with commercial condo units. In fact, just about any combination you can imagine is now possible.

Large, planned communities have been established throughout the country, with neighborhood condo projects bound with other forms of ownership under a master "umbrella" community association. Unit owners may find themselves members of two associations, one formed primarily to maintain the exteriors of their buildings and the other formed to maintain parks and recreational centers common to several projects. The costs of all such factors need to be weighed in determining what you can afford.

Condominium Financing

In many ways, financing the purchase of a condo is similar to financing a single-family home. However, some differences are worth noting. Condo advertisements for newly built or newly converted units that offer "low-rate mortgages" are common. They frequently offer below-market rates as incentives to get you to buy. This usually means the seller or developer and a lender have struck a deal in which the seller agrees to subsidize low-cost loans by paying a few percentage points. This is called a *buy-down*. It can be a good deal, but be sure to read the fine print.

If you are considering a buy-down, ask specific questions. For example, the average buy-down lasts from one to five years. After that period, the seller ends the subsidy and the interest rate returns to the market level. Be sure to ask whether the loan continues in effect after the buy-down expires or whether you will have to find another loan.

You should also ask about the terms of any continued

financing you may be locked into. Will it be a fixed rate? An adjustable rate? A rate that is a few points above market? (These rates are defined in Chapter 9.)

COOPERATIVES

There are some important differences between condominiums and cooperatives, or co-ops. The main distinction is that you actually purchase real estate when you buy a condominium; you obtain a deed and must pay your own property taxes. When you buy a co-op, you are buying not the property, but stock in a corporation that owns the property. Your stock represents your ownership interest in the unit and gives you voting rights.

You will pay a monthly amount that consists of essentially three payments. The first is the loan payment against what you borrowed to buy the unit from the seller. The second part is the portion of the co-op's overriding mortgage that you as a buyer assume. The third is the monthly maintenance or "carrying" charge for upkeep, insurance, taxes and some utilities.

The corporation issues you a lease that gives you the right to occupy your unit and use the common areas. You must come up with the purchase price, usually from a bank loan, but the monthly loan payments you make to the co-op are not really payments on a mortgage; instead, you are paying off a personal loan to the corporation. You also pay no real estate taxes directly; the corporation pays these, but in figuring your income taxes, you can deduct that part of your co-op or residence fee that is used to pay property taxes.

Your co-op fee may seem a lot like rent, but it is actually nothing at all like it. When you pay rent, you buy a service: the right to live on someone else's property. Once you use the service, you can't get your money back. When you pay your co-op fee, however, you are paying for services: maintenance of the property, repairs, utilities, and so on. Also, as you pay off the purchase price of your unit, it may seem like rent, but it's more like a mortgage: you are investing in ownership and accumulating the salable value of what you own—your equity in the corporation's stock. Afterwards you have something you can sell, with the hope of getting some or all of your investment back—or more.

Co-ops are popular in certain areas of the country and virtually unheard of in others. Because what you are really buying into is a corporation and not a piece of real estate, many of the government protections and regulations that apply to ownership of real property do not apply. This allows the co-op's board to be more selective in its choice of whom it permits to live on the property. You will have to be approved by the board of directors that governs the co-op. This process can be pro forma, involving only disclosure of your financial stability as proof that you can afford to live there, or it can involve a personal profile, references of past residences and a personal interview.

This selection process is as important to you as it is to the co-op board. You will want to learn as much about the building, the association management and other owners as you can. The section of this book on "Questions to Ask" (page 14) offers a few tips on choosing a particular co-op to live in.

Cooperative Financing

The difference between the legal structures of cooperatives and condominiums has important consequences. For one thing, it's often harder to borrow money for a co-op than for a condo, mostly because the co-op buyer receives a corporate stock certificate instead of a deed. The buyer therefore doesn't have the same physical collateral to offer the lender as insurance that the loan will be paid on time.

Because co-op buyers have no deed to offer as collateral, their loans are usually considered more as personal loans than home mortgages. In such cases, lenders are more likely to examine a borrower's credit record closely and require a higher down payment than they might for a loan backed up by the deed to the property being bought.

Also, because payment of taxes, some utilities and other assessments on the property will be out of your control, lenders may want to get a more detailed analysis of your current and expected income and debts—your ability to pay back the loan. This will add to the paperwork and time it takes to approve your mortgage application.

Finally, cooperative associations are themselves financed by an overriding, or "blanket," mortgage for the whole co-op. When you buy into a co-op, you tie yourself directly to the other owners: you incur a share of their overall debt. To the lender you ask for a loan, this will mean evaluating much more than your own financial profile. The bank will also want to look at the co-op's financial profile. This is the reason lenders are sometimes reluctant to make mortgages for co-ops and the reason many co-op boards are very selective about whom to accept as a buyer. A co-op with a reputation for having only the most qualified and reliable owners will have an easier time getting financing for its own needs.

Lenders have responded to all this with "share financing," especially in areas where co-ops are prevalent. This allows you to obtain a mortgage for the cost of your co-op based on the overriding mortgage of the entire co-op. You are really getting what would otherwise be known as a second mortgage, one based on the equity in an existing mortgage.

When co-ops first entered the market, the real estate industry found it hard to adapt. Things are somewhat better now, especially in areas where co-ops are popular. One major adjustment was made by the secondary mortgage market, which purchases loans from mortgage companies, banks and other lenders. Some of the large companies that "buy" loans to sell to secondary lenders (for instance, "Fannie Mae"), now purchase co-op loans, making more lenders less reluctant to make these loans to co-op buyers. But it may still take some looking.

Again, if you are thinking of buying a co-op, remember to look closely not only at the co-op loan rate, but also at the monthly maintenance fees. You have no accurate way of predicting how high or how fast these fees will rise, but if you examine past trends in the development, you may get an idea of what to expect.

QUESTIONS TO ASK

Buying a condominium or co-op ties your fate to the actions of others—your fellow members of the condo association or fellow stockholders of the co-op corporation. Before buying, you will want to know as much as possible about the way the association or corporation is run and how its decisions are made. You especially need to know whether you will be free to sell and get out if you become displeased and whether you'll be charged a penalty for doing so.

Read the articles of incorporation and bylaws of the co-op corporation. You will be given a copy to read and often will be asked to sign a statement certifying that you have read them. If you're not automatically given these documents, insist on seeing them. Many standard contracts and state laws require disclosure of these documents as well as past and future budgets. They also require a "contingency" that is not released until you've certified that you've had a chance to read them. Finally, you should receive a letter certifying whether the unit's assessments are paid in full.

Read the governing papers of the association. How is the board of directors elected? How long do directors serve? What does it take to remove them from office? Are you bound by every decision they make? On what matters do non–board members get to vote? How much say will you have over who gets the contracts for things like fuel and maintenance work? All of these questions should be answered fully *before you buy.*

You should also get a financial picture of the corporation: budgets, minutes of meetings, planned future expenses, lists of special assessments, copies or descriptions of outstanding mortgages or loans, engineers' reports from past or projected repairs or renovations. Talk to the co-op or condo treasurer.

Finally, it is a good idea to learn what you can about the aspirations and tendencies of the condo or co-op board. You will want to know whether its members are thrifty or extravagant and will want to get a sense of how they have been spending (or not spending) the association's money. The last thing you want is to move into a co-op or condo where the board decides to redecorate the lobby each time a new president is elected. You can get a sense of this by looking at previous as well as current budgets and by talking to real estate agents who are familiar with the property, the other owners and the current officers.

Here are some things to pay particular attention to:

- What are the fees? All of them? How often are assessments made?
- How large a down payment is required? This is especially important and restrictive in co-ops, not only for you; it also bears on whether you'll have trouble finding a buyer when you want to sell.
- How large a reserve does the association maintain? Are there plans to increase or deplete it dramatically?
- Are there limits on what you can do to your unit in terms of remodeling? Painting? Air-conditioning? Shrubbery? Satellite dishes? Room additions? Appliances?
- Does the association have any "rights of first refusal"? Do you have to sell your unit to the association if it matches any offer made by another buyer? (This could mean trou-

ble finding a buyer, who may not want to go through the trouble of tendering an offer only to have the association buy the unit instead.

- What are the limits on your ability to rent out your unit? On whom you can sell to? On whether you can have house guests?
- Is the property restricted to owner-occupied units? Many buildings stipulate that only owners are allowed to live there. Others let owners rent their property but only for a limited time or permit only a certain number of units to be rented. Some association boards believe resident-owners tend to take better care of the property than owners who buy units to use as rental property. If residence is not restricted to owners, you can use the property as an investment or source of rental income.
- Are there limits on pets, children, whether you can marry (in the case of "singles" condos)?

Condo and co-op buyers are usually given estimates of the expenses of owning the unit, including all fees and estimates of utilities. Remember, these are subject to change. Indeed, it is wise to assume they will increase, especially in the case of new developments or newly converted units.

When a developer or seller misrepresents the actual costs of operating a condo unit, it is called "low-balling." Victims of this tactic have successfully sued developers in several cases.

INTRODUCTORY OFFERS

In some developments the condominium fee is waived for an introductory period or kept artificially low to attract buyers.

It's wise always to be wary of introductory incentives, especially the most attractive ones. They often look better than they are. Low introductory fees can climb rapidly once the designated period is over, and there is little you can do to prevent it. One reason is that many of the expenses paid out of the fees—utility bills, for example—are out of the control of the condo association. The best you can do is look for a condo that has a reputation for being frugal (but not too frugal to let important maintenance tasks slip by) when it comes to assessments against the unit owners.

CONDO/CO-OP CONVERSIONS

Many people find themselves in the position of having to decide whether to buy a home without ever wanting one and without being prepared. This is because the building or development where they are renting is undergoing a "conversion" to a condo or co-op. Many states have laws that govern when rental property can be converted by a developer or owner.

Generally, the laws were passed either to preserve low-income rental housing in the community or to give existing tenants the "right of first refusal" to purchase their unit or, sometimes, another unit in the building at a below-market price. If you find yourself in this position, look closely at the offer you're being given, learn your rights under your state's law and pay careful attention not to miss the deadlines for action or notices on your part. After the initial offer and your acceptance, most of the transaction will proceed much like the sale of any other condo or co-op. Tenants usually, at this point, form an association to investigate the offer, the conditions and their mutual interests.

All tenants will receive a notice of the owner's intention to convert and an offer to buy a unit at a below-market price. This offer is known as a "red herring." The laws typically work so that if a certain percentage of residents accept the offer to buy or "convert," then the building can go co-op. In some states those who don't accept will be forced to move, but a provision in many laws protects residents by giving them the right to remain in the building as renters if the building goes co-op and they do not want to buy.

Before you accept a purchase-price offer, compare yours with other tenants' and get a statement in writing about any restrictions on your right to sell within a certain period of time.

CONDO/CO-OP WARRANTIES

If you're buying a newly constructed condo or co-op, you will need to know about your protection under warranties. Warranties are legally enforceable assurances about the quality or condition of a property or its appliances and systems. They can be in the form of a contract between two parties or an across-the-board pledge. They can be imposed by states or by the federal government. Warranties under one federal law, the Magnuson-Moss Warranty Act, apply to such things as appliances and furnaces in new homes, and a clause in your contract will reflect this.

The same warranties that are available to purchasers of single-family houses (see Chapter 7) are available to purchasers of condos and co-ops. These include direct warranties by the builder as well as guarantees by contractors or manufacturers of components and appliances. These latter warranties are rarely revealed until the title is obtained, however. At the least you should make sure the purchase contract provides for delivery of all warranties at the closing (see Chapter 14). Also, be sure to purchase insurance if you want to make sure you're covered if something not covered by a warranty breaks down during the first year of ownership.

Specifically ask for certain warranties that are frequently omitted from the purchase contract or through failure to deliver separate written guarantees. These include warranties for kitchen cabinets, bathroom vanities, flooring, air-conditioning ducts, wrought ironwork, roofing, siding, concrete work other than foundations, electrical systems and painting. While reputable builders usually insist that the subcontractors they hire provide them with effective warranties covering defects in materials or installation, the terms and application of those obligations are rarely expressed in the buyer's contract or even worded in favor of the buyer.

Be sure also to look for warranties that cover things outside your own dwelling unit. Correcting defects in parking lot pavement, elevators or swimming pool installations will have to be paid for by you and the other unit owners unless you have warranties.

A SPECIAL NOTE

If you plan to use a lawyer* or other professional in buying a condo or co-op, start early. Purchasing a unit requires reviews of the contract, all warranties and the condominium association or corporation papers. No one can be expected to digest and evaluate all these documents at the last moment. If you want help, get it early to avoid last-minute delays or surprises.

*See *Using A Lawyer* by Kay Ostberg in association with HALT, Random House, 1990.

CHAPTER **3**

PROFESSIONALS

The real estate industry supports a wide variety of professionals who, for a fee, provide just as wide a variety of services. They include brokers and agents, mortgage bankers, developers, investors, financial planners, appraisers, escrow agents and, of course, lawyers. You may never need any of them or you may need them all, but you will be better off if you understand what they offer—and where their interests lie. Only then will you be able to participate confidently in decision making.

Even if you decide to proceed on your own or work only with one or two professionals, you should be familiar with the roles they all play—because the seller may have hired them.

SELLERS' REAL ESTATE BROKERS AND AGENTS

Brokers are professionals who find prospective buyers for a seller's home. *Agents* usually work for brokers. Both must pass a test to be licensed. Both work for the seller, not the buyer. Realtors are real estate brokers who belong to the National Association of Realtors—a trade association of 800,000 real estate professionals.

Some people acquire a real estate license but work only

as part-time agents or brokers to supplement income from their full-time careers; others do it full time. Be aware that some part-timers may be far less knowledgeable or connected to the local market or available than their full-time counterparts.

People who want to sell their homes contract brokers to advertise and secure ready, willing and qualified buyers. This is called *listing* the home with a broker. The listing can be either "exclusive," meaning the seller is restricted from looking elsewhere for a buyer for a specified period, or open and unrestricted. Some sellers include a "reserve" clause in their contract with the broker, giving them the right to find a buyer on their own. If they do find a buyer without the broker's help, they do not have to pay the broker anything. If you know that a seller can avoid paying a commission to a broker, either because of a reserve clause or because the home is "for sale by owner," you may be able to negotiate a lower price.

Multiple Listing Service

Many brokers work through a *multiple listing service* operated by local real estate associations. This is a computer bank of homes that are on the market. It describes their characteristics, price and other features. Most brokers have access to these listings, and a seller who uses a broker often includes in the contract that the home will be listed with the "multiples," as it is called in the trade. This method gives the seller a much broader pool of potential buyers and usually means the home will sell faster (see Chapter 5).

Commissions

If the broker finds a buyer and the deal goes through, he or she collects a percentage of the purchase price, called a *commission,* from the seller. As a buyer, you can go to a broker, be shown every home on the market, and pay nothing for the service. Be aware, however, that if you buy a house this way, the broker's commission is probably already included in the price you're paying. In effect, the seller doesn't pay the broker, you do.

The broker who signs the contract with the seller is called the "listing" broker or agent. If this broker finds a buyer, he or she is paid the full commission the seller negotiated and contracted for, usually 4% to 7% of the purchase price.

If another broker produces a buyer either by using the multiples or by bringing a buyer to an "open house," the listing broker still gets a commission but has to split it with the broker who produced the buyer. This person is sometimes called the "secondary" broker. Mostly because of the multiples, splitting commissions has become widespread.

Broker Loyalty

One caution: although brokers can provide a valuable service to prospective home buyers by saving them the irritation of having to search on their own, it is not the broker's job to guarantee that you get the best price or that the property has no problems or defects. That's your job or a responsibility you can hire others to handle.

Many people think that because a broker escorts them to homes and gives them information about a seller that sounds like advice or inside knowledge, the broker is working for them. This is a grave mistake. Even though they may call themselves "your" broker, they are not working for you but for the seller. This distinction gets even more blurred in buyers' minds when two brokers are involved—a quite common occurrence.

In the eyes of the law, brokers are responsible only for representations they themselves make. Of course, happy customers make for a better reputation and the broker does have an incentive for getting you to buy the home: it's called the commission. Thus, if a broker has an interest in satisfying you, it's a publicity and marketing decision, not an enforceable legal duty. Although your interests may correspond to those of the broker to some extent, don't assume they do in all aspects of the deal. The bottom line is that the loyalties of both the listing and the secondary broker run to the seller, not the buyer.

BUYER'S AGENTS

A positive trend for home buyers is the recent rise in the popularity of *buyer's agents.* A buyer's agent is paid an hourly or flat fee determined before you begin shopping for a home. Because the fee is known beforehand and is not based on the price of the property, the agent has no incentive to push you toward a more expensive property. Some buyer's agents, however, may encourage you to have them split the commission with the seller's broker. In other words, the more you pay, the higher the fee. As you can imagine, such an arrangement is not to your advantage.

The U.S. Department of Housing and Urban Development (HUD) encourages home buyers to explore a buyer's agent arrangement because of its potential for improving the quality and integrity of services. One of the advantages is that you have an all-purpose consultant—if you shop around and hire a good one. A buyer's agent can go with you on house-hunting trips, review or even negotiate your contract, tour the home with you to look for defects, examine the management and financial records of the condo or co-op association, help with financing and be at your side for the closing.

And, unlike a seller's agent, there's no confusion about which side the loyalty runs to. A buyer's agent is on *your* side.

Don't be surprised if agents don't know what you are talking about when you ask them to be your buyer's agent. In many parts of the country, most agents have not picked up on this trend. Whatever you do, shop around, be clear that you are looking for a *buyer's* agent and get the best price.

APPRAISERS

Before buying a house, you will want one or more people to judge its value so you can know whether the asking price is fair. Professionals who do this for a living are called *appraisers.* Any prospective buyer can have an appraisal done at any time. When you hire a professional appraiser to give you an objective valuation of the property, you can be reasonably sure the person is not on anyone's "side" and has no common interest either with you or the seller. The professional is merely selling a service.

Sometimes two appraisals are done for the same home sale because some lenders, banks for example, require a separate appraisal before approving a loan. It's a good idea to check first with your prospective lender to make sure the appraisal company you choose is acceptable. Many people have only one appraisal done—the lender's. The choice is yours and you can save money following that route, but if you're at all suspicious of collusion, have an independent appraisal done by someone of *your* choosing.

LENDERS

Banks, savings and loans, insurance companies, union pension funds, credit unions, and other lending institutions can all provide you with the money to buy a home (see Chapter 10). At this point you need to know only that, unlike appraisers, lenders have a direct interest in the deal you strike and the quality of the property you buy. If, in the future, you fail to make your loan payments (*default*), the lender will take your home (*foreclose*) and sell it to regain the lost money. That's why the lender wants to make sure you are buying a home that can be resold for at least as much as the amount of the loan you're asking.

Although lenders do have an interest in the value of the property, don't expect them to be your allies. For all practical purposes, lenders don't really care if you pay an inflated price for a house. They care only that, if you default, they can make up their losses.

ESCROW AGENTS

An *escrow agent* arranges all the paperwork, documents and payments involved in a house closing. Sometimes the escrow agent is a real estate broker, agent or lawyer, sometimes an uninvolved professional. The term escrow refers to the depositing of money or documents with a neutral party who has a duty to hold them until certain conditions are met. Where an escrow agent performs the closing tasks, that agent is responsible for holding all of the documents until all promises are fulfilled, at which time the money is released and the necessary papers filed.

LAWYERS

More than any of the other professionals, lawyers are the ones you hire to look after your interests each step of the way. They have a duty to watch over your interests, but be cautious: what they do for you depends on the terms of your agreement.

You can hire an experienced real estate lawyer for any or all of the following services: to draft or review your purchase contract; to negotiate with the seller or the seller's agent; to check that the appraisals are not unrealistically high or low;

to conduct the title search; and to attend the closing with you (see Chapter 13). At the least, many buyers rely on lawyers to do the *title search,* a check to be sure that there are no conflicting claims or problems with the ownership of your property (see Chapter 12).

However, even in the present complex real estate market, more and more people are routinely buying homes without the help of lawyers, especially people who are buying their first home, those with no existing home to sell and those considering a home that is under the "conforming mortgage" limit. This is a limit, set by the large companies in the secondary mortgage market, that ranges around $170,000–$180,000 (see under "Secondary Mortgage Market" in Chapter 10).

The trend toward buying a home without a lawyer is occurring despite charges by state and local bars that nonlawyer agents who draw up real estate contracts are guilty of the unauthorized practice of law. As more and more agents defy such threats and perform functions traditionally reserved for lawyers, both buyers and sellers save money.

Clearer laws, plain-language requirements and more efficient government agencies and processes will enable still more people to purchase their homes without the additional expense of hiring legal counsel. While we wait for the government to act on these reforms, however, buyers who do proceed on their own are cautioned to utilize every resource that is available and to be well-informed shoppers.

Many people hire an all-purpose real estate law firm to do all their paperwork and make sure the transaction complies with the law. This is especially true when people sell their home without a broker and need a neutral party to act on their behalf.

Large real estate companies also may offer this service through a local law firm, and they will undoubtedly let you know about this when you sign the contract. Using such services can save you some money, because the fee is decided in advance and split by the parties. One caution, however: make sure the company is acting as a neutral "closing" agent and not working for either side in the sale.

WHO COSTS WHAT?

Sellers' brokers and agents are paid on commission. They receive a percentage of the price of the home when they provide a ready, willing and qualified buyer. The rate usually ranges from 4% to 7%. If two brokers are involved—a listing broker and a secondary broker—they split the commission, usually down the middle. (They, not you, will negotiate their percentage.)

Keep in mind that brokers and agents who work for real estate firms routinely turn half their commission over to the company to cover overhead, including office space, telephone, and advertising. This doesn't affect your price, but it's important to know that often only half the commission goes to the broker. If a deal has two brokers and one of them works for a company, that broker can end up with only a quarter of the total commission.

Buyer's agents can be paid an hourly, flat or percentage fee, depending on the deal you negotiate. Shop around to get the best price and be aware of the possible conflict of interest that can arise from a commission arrangement (page 23).

Appraisers are paid by the buyer, either a flat fee or a commission based on the property's selling price.

Lenders are paid by charging "points," a percent of the loan, and other fees. These will be disclosed to you in advance (see Chapter 9).

Escrow (or closing) agents' fees are usually split between the buyer and seller. If the escrow agent is one of the parties working for the buyer or seller, many of the closing costs—for example, document preparation—will be paid, usually in a flat fee, to that agent.

Lawyers usually charge a flat fee for a specified range of services, including the title search, contract review, overseeing some of the inspections, doing a final walk-through inspection of the property to check its condition, preparing some or all of the documents and attending the closing. Their fees range from $200 to $1,000. Be sure to get a written lawyer-client contract that spells out what services* are included and at what cost to you.

*See *Using a Lawyer* by Kay Ostberg in association with HALT, Random House, 1990.

CHAPTER 4

BENEFITS
AND COSTS

Before you begin shopping, weigh the benefits and burdens of homeownership in light of your goals, life-style and financial and other commitments. This will give you an idea of your home-buying potential. You may or may not want to ask the help of one or more professionals—a financial planner or real estate counselor—but read the rest of this chapter first. It may convince you that you can do all or most of the evaluation yourself.

THE BENEFITS

Building Equity

Homeownership is part of the American dream, an investment for the future. Regardless of how reasonable your rent, paying it does nothing to help your financial future. It is money spent and gone. Even though interest rates may be high, many people are attracted to the idea of having a home in which to build *equity*. Equity is that part of the home's value that is yours, the part you would keep if you sold the home and then paid off what was left of your mortgage. The idea is that with each mortgage payment, your equity in the property increases as it does with increases in the market value.

A major question for many people who want to buy a

home is whether they should do it now and settle for less than their dream house or wait until they are better established financially and can get the real thing. Caution never hurts, but the idea behind equity is that money paid into a mortgage, less interest, will almost always be recovered upon sale of the home even though the full mortgage hasn't been paid off. (In fact, few people, unless they live in the same house for twenty or thirty years, pay off an entire mortgage without first selling the home.) Thus, buying a small "starter house" now could well be a springboard to buying a better one later. Under present tax regulations, you don't have to pay income taxes on the profit you make selling your present home if you reinvest it in another home within two years.

One warning: under certain circumstances homeownership may be a dream that can make you poor. Many people scrimp and save to make a down payment on a house, then tie themselves to a mortgage they can barely afford. As a result, they have no spare money for the things they once enjoyed—movies, vacations, sports, dinners out. Be careful to compare your desire to own a home with the risk of being "house poor."

Tax Breaks

Having a mortgage to pay can be a particular advantage if you need or want to shelter some of your income from taxes. At present, all the interest you pay on the mortgage can be deducted, dollar for dollar, from your income when calculating your income taxes. This is an especially big and early bonus to those whose mortgages are structured so that most of the first few years' payments are interest (see Chapter 9).

Building Credit

Maintaining a mortgage also builds your credit capability. Although you tie up a lot of cash in a home purchase, you will be allowed to borrow money based on the amount of the loan you've paid off. As a result, each year that you make all the payments on time, new credit doors will open if you need them.

Inheritance

As a homeowner, you can pass most types of ownership on to your heirs. Also, by selecting carefully from among the forms of ownership discussed in Chapter 1, you can set up the ownership so that it avoids probate.

WHAT CAN YOU AFFORD?

The most important element of buying a home is how much you can afford. Lenders will ultimately make the decision for you by deciding whether to give you a mortgage. Without a mortgage, few people can afford a home. While lenders do consider whether you seem reliable, most of their decision is based on cold calculations of your assets and income.

Each lender has a different formula, and even within one company, how this decision is made can vary depending on the type of loan you're applying for and the size of your down payment. A good rule of thumb is that you will not be approved for a loan if the monthly payments, including taxes and fees, exceed 25% to 30% of your income. There are exceptions, but this is a good yardstick to keep in mind.

Secondary Loan Market

Most mortgage loans are "sold" immediately after the closing to large companies in what is known as the secondary or conforming loan market (Fannie Mae and Freddie Mac are two institutions that buy loans from lenders for sale to the large investors on the secondary market). Virtually all lenders use the guidelines issued by these companies to determine whether to give you a mortgage. A conforming loan is one under an amount that has been about $187,000 and that conforms to the following standards:

- That no more than 28% of your monthly income is used for your mortgage (25% if your down payment is less than 10% of the cost of the home)
- That no more than 36% of your income is used to pay regular debts (33% if your down payment is less than 10% of the cost of the home)
- If you apply for an FHA mortgage, you have more flexibility: 29% of your income can service the loan and 41% of your income can be used for other debts

Analyze your financial potential rationally, the way a lender will, so you won't be found financially unqualified *after* you have begun negotiating for the home you want. Calculating what you can afford is the first and most important step. How well you do it determines how well your investment will turn out.

Many home buyers rely on the lender to put their financial picture together for them. This can lead to problems down the road—even outright disaster—because too many lenders may not know or care whether you are committing yourself to spending more than you can comfortably afford. After all, their interest is in getting *their* money's worth, not yours. The two goals aren't necessarily the same.

Try very hard to weigh and consider *all* your expenses, including hidden ones. A lender will ask about fixed monthly expenses, bills, tuition, car payments, even transportation expenses, but you will have to include and determine for yourself the "style of life" expenses that will cut into what you have left after these essentials. These include recreation, hobbies, movie and theater tickets, dining out and travel. Unless you factor these in, you will end up with a skewed idea of what your budget can absorb.

Start Early

It's worth saying again that the search for a loan is at least as important as the search for a home. Because of this, you should start the search *at the same time* you begin to look for your dream house. Talk to people who have done it before. Talk to banks, friends, relatives, colleagues at work. Build a list of possible sources of loans, what seems to be the going interest rate, lengths of loans and any other facts you think pertinent.

The "Up-Front" Costs

Try to arrive at a good estimate of the total cost of buying a home. Be sure to count fees for professional services, inspections, adjustments, closing costs, homeowner's insurance, property taxes, utilities and maintenance. In many instances, what these fees are will depend on the price range of the home you're considering, but they can be estimated ahead of time. (Chapters 7–14 will help you make these estimates.)

In addition, you may also need cash for furniture, appliances and other household items. Be sure to include them in your list because they can add up to a significant outlay.

The Down Payment

The largest single item you'll have to pay is probably the down payment, the amount of cash the lender wants "up front" against the purchase price *before* a loan is made. This sum reduces the amount of the loan. For example, if the home costs $100,000, the lender will likely require a minimum down payment of $20,000, leaving a mortgage balance of $80,000 to be paid over time. Depending on market conditions, the size of the minimum down payment usually varies from 10% to 25% of the purchase price.

Alternatively, it can be as low as 5% for housing in the lower price range that qualifies for an FHA loan, and no down payment is required for veterans receiving VA loans (see Chapter 10).

When interest rates are low and stable, it makes sense to put as little cash "down" as possible and to borrow the rest. That way, if interest rates go up during the life of your loan, you'll be in a good position paying the low rate. With higher and more volatile interest rates, it is wise to borrow as little as possible. Nevertheless, such decisions depend on your personal financial situation. If, for example, tax savings are very important to you, you may want a large loan so as to use the interest payments to reduce your income tax.

YOUR NET WORTH

After you add up all the cash outlays you can expect to make before moving into your new home, it's time to calculate your net worth. This is particularly useful in determining how much cash you can afford to put down on a home. Your net worth is arrived at by totaling all your assets and subtracting your debts. You will need this information before making any important decisions, so it's best to get it out of the way early. Besides, your lender is going to require it anyway.

Your calculations tell you how much money you have available for your down payment and other up-front expenses. Remember, you may have to use some of this money for other moving-in expenses, too, so be cautious. Subtract from your net worth all of your estimated fees, expenses and moving costs.

Now evaluate how much cash reserve your particular family needs. A college fund? Vacation money? A reserve for uncovered medical expenses? Money for orthodonture? For a computer course? Calculate such possibilities for your own situation. Then ask yourself: How much money do I need in the bank to keep me from feeling I am off to the poorhouse?

Subtract these estimates from your net worth and you will know what down payment you can actually handle. Use the following worksheet to get started:

NET WORTH WORKSHEET
as of _____
(date)

ASSETS

Bank account balance(s) (checking, savings)	_____
Stocks	_____
Bonds	_____
Insurance (cash value)	_____
Certificate(s) of deposit	_____
Accounts receivable (cash-in value owed to you)	_____
Real estate (appraised value)	_____
Automobile(s), boats, planes (resale value)	_____
Personal property (antiques, jewelry, furs, silver, china)	_____
Annuity(ies) (surrender value)	_____
Other assets	_____
TOTAL ASSETS	_____

LIABILITIES

Debts to banks and other lenders (nonmortgage and auto loans)	_____
Real estate mortgage(s) (balance due)	_____
Outstanding credit card account bills	_____
Unpaid income taxes	_____
Auto and other vehicle loan(s) (balance due)	_____
Personal debts	_____
Other debts	_____
TOTAL LIABILITIES	_____
TOTAL ASSETS (from above)	_____

LESS TOTAL LIABILITIES   _____
LESS "RESERVE"   _____
NET WORTH   _____

Monthly Income

After calculating the down payment you can afford, the next step is to determine how much you can afford to pay each month on your mortgage. Unless you're applying for a government-backed loan, the lender will usually trust your estimate of your cost of living. To figure your monthly income and expenses, list all sources of income: salaries, interest, stock dividends, trust payments, pensions, rental income, royalties, alimony, child support, and so on. Then list all expenses: food, clothing, recreation, transportation, charities, installment payments, credit card bills, dues, entertainment, and so on. If you calculate well, you will have determined how much you have available for monthly mortgage payments.

A word of caution: lenders will be particularly sensitive to large monthly payments you are already making and will use them to reduce their estimate of the monthly payment they will approve for you. For example, if you are paying $200 a month on your car, some lenders will reduce their estimate of what additional loans you can handle by twice that amount or more. To be attractive to lenders and realistic with yourself, it's a good idea to rid yourself of as many monthly payments as you can and plan to keep new commitments low.

Your total monthly payments for housing—including mortgage, taxes, insurance, utilities, maintenance and repairs—should not be more than 25% to 30% of your monthly income. Of course, this figure is subject to your specific circumstances and your lender's requirements.

Before making this calculation, check whether your mortgage estimate includes taxes on the property. Many people "escrow" their taxes, which means the mortgage company adds this to the monthly payments and pays the taxes to the government for the homeowner at the appropriate time. Make sure you don't forget these taxes or double-count them.

HOW TO FIGURE MONTHLY MORTGAGE COSTS

To estimate how much you can afford each month, you need some fancy mathematics. It is not simply a matter of taking the total mortgage, calculating the interest and dividing by the number of payments. This is because loans are "amortized," meaning that each year's declining balance and the interest on the balance are added up and then divided by the number of payments.

You can find an amortization table for mortgages in some real estate books, in guidebooks for realtors and in some accounting books. The tables provide the interest rate and the number of years of the mortgage. They then use a "multiplier" you use with the number of thousands of dollars in your mortgage. Some pocket calculators have the table already programmed. Or you can ask your loan officer to calculate the figure for you.

YOUR CREDIT RATING

All this calculating may be in vain if there is a credit "skeleton in your closet." You can be sure that if it's there, your lender will find it. It's one of the things lenders do best.

Check your credit report *before* beginning the search for financing. You can get the information from your local credit reporting agency for a small fee. However, because the efficiency of reporting systems varies greatly, it's wise to ask a few major lending institutions in your community where they go for residential loan credit reviews.

If you have had problems with one or more creditors in the past, try to reach an understanding with them. If you feel you have been treated unfairly, write a well-documented letter supporting your position and file it with your local credit bureau *before* you apply for a mortgage.

Lenders are especially concerned about prior bankruptcy judgments, court collection judgments, garnishment of wages, attachment of assets and defaults on prior loans. These are what make "red flags" go up; 99% of the time, any such problems in your past will spell automatic denial of your mortgage application. A few late or missed payments on loans, overdue credit card balances and even a bill being sent to a collection agency may not spell automatic denial, but needless to say, they can't help.

Sometimes, however, such matters are not even reported or listed on a credit reference service's report. For example, action against you by a collection agency may not be reported to the credit bureau or to the lender requesting the report unless a lawsuit is filed against you and you lose. To make sure what will and what will not cause a problem, get a copy of your credit report before the lender does, then be prepared either to make good on your debts or explain them convincingly.

CHAPTER 5

HOUSE HUNTING

Now that you have determined what kind of down payment and monthly loan payments you can afford, you can begin looking seriously for a home. The way to ensure that you find the best is to plan carefully, follow your plan and exhaust all options.

Begin by drawing a clear picture of the kind of home you're looking for. Make a list of the characteristics of places you have liked and disliked. Then rank these characteristics as "musts," "options" and "dreams."

For instance, a "must" may be two bathrooms if you have a large family, or off-street parking if you're moving to the center of a city. An "option" may be a fireplace, a terrace or a kitchen pantry. A "dream" may be a greenhouse, skylights, a health club or a roof deck. After making your list, think about where you will compromise.

Be Extravagant In the world of real estate, just about everything is negotiable. For you this means that, in the beginning, nothing should be ruled out. Even the highest-priced house in the wealthiest neighborhood may be within your reach—for example, if it needs work, or if the owner needs to sell quickly. Now is the time to let yourself be a little extravagant.

Get Started Early The more time you have, the better. If you start your search well before making a commitment to move out of your current home, you have the luxury of being free to take your time. If you can do this, you won't have to live with the uncertainty of not knowing whether you bought the right house or apartment.

Plan Your Search If you have defined your housing requirements accurately and fully, you are in a position to make the best use of real estate guidebooks and home-buying seminars and avoid hit-and-miss hunting techniques. Attending one or more community classes on home buying can be particularly helpful, considering how the process varies from one place to another. Check the bibliography (Appendix IV) for other resources.

WHAT ARE YOU LOOKING FOR?

You need to make decisions on where you want to live and what kind of property you want. Consider the kind of neighborhood—city, suburban or rural—and the proximity to services and amenities like schools, shopping, places of worship and transportation. Next think about such questions as the number of bedrooms, bathrooms and closets, yard space, terrace, separate dining areas and so on. (Many such considerations are listed in the discussion of inspections in Chapter 7.) Make your decisions now based on the ideal—your "dream" house—then weigh them against what is realistic after you start seeing what's available in your price range. Here are some questions to ask when you're looking for the right neighborhood:

- Do you want a detached home, a town house or an apartment?
- Are you interested only in new homes? Do you want to live in a development that has recreational facilities?
- What kind of neighborhood are you looking for? Quiet? With shops, restaurants and atmosphere?

- Do you have children or plan to have them soon? Do you need a home near a playground or away from dangerous traffic? Will you need a place to walk the dog?
- What is the crime rate?
- How far are the school, bus or subway line, grocery store, dry cleaner, hardware store and place of worship?
- How is the parking?
- How good are city services? Will you pay extra for trash collection?
- Are the real estate values likely to rise or decline?

It's also a good idea to ask your prospective neighbors what they think about the neighborhood, development or building. Ask about the rate of commercial development, whether house break-ins are common, the level of police activity, how far you are from a thoroughfare for emergency vehicles. Ask these questions of people who have no direct interest in having you move there. A seller's broker can answer some questions, but be sure to check with neighbors, shopkeepers and even the local police. Brokers want to make the sale and will paint the best picture possible. You want a more critical analysis.

Once you know what kind of neighborhood you're looking for and have narrowed your search to a specific community, you're ready to find a home for sale.

Check Classified Ads The want ads provide a survey of the entire community, a cross-section of the day-to-day offerings in the residential market, an idea of prices, and a sense of what various neighborhoods are like. The ads are often divided into separate sections for detached houses, condominiums and co-ops. Saturdays and Sundays are the best days to look for ads, although they do run on other days and some papers make a point of advertising homes for sale on Friday to get ahead of the competition.

Checking the real estate ads daily for a few weeks will give you an idea of how quickly properties are sold, the prices being asked and which the dominant real estate companies are.

Classified ads take some skill to decipher. If you're having trouble, you can find out what all the abbreviations mean by calling the classified ad section of the newspaper or consulting a real estate agent. Be aware that these ads are intended to lure you into calling, so it is important to read them carefully. Don't get your hopes up until you see the property being advertised or at least talk to the seller or the seller's agent.

In any case, you'll have to telephone to get information that isn't in the ads. Before calling sellers and agents, be sure to compile a written list of important questions based on your listed "musts," "options" and "dreams."

Attend Open Houses   To narrow down your list of what's important, list what you like and don't like in your current home, even if it's rented. Then go to "open houses" and get a feel for the market. These are hours during which anyone, with or without a broker, can tour a property that is on the market. In many parts of the country, when sellers contract with a real estate broker, they arrange for a certain number of open houses.

Where they are used, open houses are advertised in the newspaper, usually for the weekends. They are indicated by real estate company signs out front of the property and, sometimes, a block or so away, directing passersby. If your search is limited to a relatively small area, you can probably just stroll around looking for such signs. Especially in the high selling seasons of spring, summer and early fall, it's not unusual to find one or two residences for sale on any city block. If you're looking in a suburban or rural area, you will want to check the classified ads first, then narrow your driving time by getting directions to the homes you want to see.

During each open house, ask questions that will help you

understand the home-buying process and differentiate among your musts, options and dreams. Some questions you might ask are:

- Do you have a fact sheet on the property? This will give you the basic information, including square footage, age of appliances and systems (plumbing and electrical), and type of ownership (condo, co-op or single family).
- How long has the property been on the market?
- How many square feet are there?
- Have major renovations been done recently?
- What kind of floor is under the carpeting?
- What is the neighborhood like?

You want to encourage give-and-take with the broker or seller to increase your sophistication and knowledge about what is and what isn't going to be acceptable and realistic when you make an offer to purchase.

After enough open-house visits, you'll be able to tell the difference between real wood floors and imitation, between ceramic tile and imitations. You'll know whether you want a kitchen large enough for dining or a separate dining area, whether you want or need a bathroom with a window. You'll look knowledgeably at closets and other storage space, finished basements, signs of water damage. You'll consider security systems, storm windows and screens, heating systems and air-conditioning. You can gain such awareness from open-house tours.

Ask Real Estate Companies   It's almost impossible to do a thorough search for a home without dealing with a broker. This is where most homeowners go when they want to sell their houses. Real estate companies offer them a place to list their homes so that a large pool of prospective buyers will hear about them. The seller signs a contract that gives the company the right to try to sell the property. The company "shows" the house and makes a sales pitch to prospective buyers. For this service, the company receives a commission—a designated, agreed-upon percentage of the sale price of the house when it is sold.

In the course of trying to make the sale, brokers can help the home buyer too. They will give information about available houses and neighborhoods, take your list of requirements and match it to houses on the market and take you to see one, two or ten houses that fit your price range and other requirements. In addition, many real estate companies publish booklets that can tell you about the local market, available financing and closing costs.

But brokers are running against the clock. If they fail to produce a ready, willing and qualified buyer within the time specified in their contract with the seller, they can lose the contract and will have wasted the time spent showing the home and talking to prospective buyers. The pressure is on them to sell the home to you, so expect all brokers to put pressure on you to get you to buy.

To find a broker to show you homes, talk to people who have done it before. Consider brokers you ran into at open houses, especially those who seemed most helpful. Look for competence and a style you like—polite, aggressive, knowledgeable about the market, well connected. Especially look for brokers who can help with connections to other aspects of home buying—financing, inspections, appraisals and title searches.

If you plan to use a real estate company, choose carefully. Select companies and agents that best suit your needs. For example, some offer discount services to their sellers, charging a flat fee instead of the usual percentage. These discount services began in the late 1980s, and the companies that offer them have prospered. They can offer these reduced costs because they allow homeowners to "show" the home themselves and help with other tasks. In return for the flat fee, the discounts provide the usual services—placing the home on the multiple listing service, providing "for sale" signs, helping with financing, etc. A discounter will charge as little as $1,000 to $1,500 to help sell a home worth less than $100,000. From the buyer's point of view, this can be beneficial if the seller is willing to pass the savings along to sell the home faster.

Some brokers are local, with deep roots in the community, others are nationwide, with listings from all over the country. Big is not necessarily better. In some cases, it may be the small, community-based broker who works best for you. Such brokers may know the area better and be able to give more in the way of a personal service than the high-volume, high-turnover companies.

THE MULTIPLE LISTING SERVICE

The *multiple listing service* (MLS) is a computerized network of homes for sale in a region. Most brokers have access to this data base. This means that in most parts of the country the MLS can put you in touch with a very large percentage of the properties on the market.

A "listing" broker puts the property on the multiple listing. This broker is under contract with the seller to sell the property in exchange for a commission. The broker who is showing homes to you, the buyer, can punch your requirements into the MLS and come up with a list of prospects. You and the broker then go to the homes you select. If you decide to make an offer, you do so through the broker who showed you the home. If the sale goes through, the broker who accompanied you splits the commission with the listing broker.

If the listing firm shows you a home it has the contract for, it in turn gets the full commission. For this reason, brokers may try to steer you first to homes they are listing to avoid splitting a commission. Nevertheless, splitting commissions has become so common that this will probably not be a problem.

If you feel you're being directed only to properties the broker has listed, consider switching. Such steering can limit your choices drastically. Be clear with brokers who show you around that you want a full showing of many homes, including those on the MLS.

YOU AND THE SELLER'S AGENT

Your relationship with an agent who represents home sellers is not one of employer to employee. It is a no-contract, informal understanding between two parties, the relationship of a customer and a salesperson in a department store. The agent hopes to sell you a property at the highest price. You hope the agent can produce a property you want and can afford.

Despite laws that bind agents to serve sellers, it is common for them to try lead buyers into believing they are looking out for the buyer's interests, too. Agents want both sides to be happy with the deals that are struck, but they are interested primarily in getting the highest commission possible. The higher the sales price, the higher that commission will be.

Agent Disclosures   Some states have passed laws requiring agents to disclose to you their relationship or "fiduciary duty" to the seller when they first start showing you homes. Members of the National Association of Realtors are also required under association rules to make such a disclosure.

One Agent or Two?   Many people question whether they are cheating one seller's agent if they also ask for help from another agent. As we've noted, agents work for the seller to produce a buyer; you have no contract or obligation to them that prevents you from working with another. In some places, local custom allows you to ask as many agents for help as you'd like, while in other places, that practice is unheard of. When you're *selling* a house, it may sometimes be to your advantage to work with an agent on an exclusive basis.

Learn what you can about the local custom from friends and other home buyers. Don't ask the brokers. They have no incentive to tell you you can also get help from their competition, even if it's true. If you do work with a second or third agent, let each one know so they don't duplicate work.

If you also plan to look for homes on your own, tell the broker who is showing you around. You especially will want to do this if you plan to look for homes that are "for sale by owner." In these cases, having an agent escort you may actually hurt your chances: the seller will not want to accept your offer because doing so may require paying the agent a commission. Avoiding such a commission is why they decided to sell the property on their own in the first place.

Here are some tips when shopping for an agent:

Start on Your Own Whether or not you plan to use real estate agents in your house hunt, it's always a good idea to shop on your own first. That way you will come to the agent with some awareness of local market conditions and what you might reasonably expect to find.

Classified ads will list houses that individual owners are selling on their own. Visit some of these, price them and educate yourself on their advantages and problems. These ads will also tell you which the major real estate companies in your area are and which seem to be listing the most homes that fit your needs. Other sources of such information include friends and relatives, people at work, neighborhood residents, supermarket bulletin boards and community organizations.

Protect Yourself It's advisable to visit several realty companies to see what properties are available in your price range. Let the agents know you understand the nature of the agency relationship and the agent's obligation to serve the seller.

Be Discreet Even though you have to give the agent some idea of your price range and your requirements, preserve your bargaining power by being discreet about what you divulge. The agent will try to gain your trust by seeming to reveal the seller's position, but be aware that the seller will hear about any weaknesses you reveal to the agent—including a need to act quickly or any overeagerness you've shown. An agent will probably ask to do a financial worksheet on you, both to be able to make offers to prospective sellers and to know the range of prices you can afford. There is no harm in doing this.

Don't Feel Pressured If an agent tells you another buyer is looking at the house today or is deciding today whether to buy the house, don't feel you have to make a quick decision. Balance your desire to buy the best home available against your need to act quickly.

Get It in Writing The law prevents agents and sellers from intentionally misrepresenting the properties they are advertising. This does not prohibit a certain amount of exaggeration, however. It's always best to have important representations about the property stated in the contract, particularly when the agent has to rely on information supplied by the seller.

A final note about the agent's commission. By law, agents' commissions are negotiable. In practice, however, they are almost always 4% to 7%. If more than one agent is involved in the purchase of your home, they will split the commission.

In theory, sellers pay these commissions, but in reality, buyers pay them because the commission is included in the sale price.

One warning merits repeating here, because you must always bear it in mind: seller's agents and brokers can help you—but they don't work for you. Your interests and theirs seldom coincide.

YOU AND THE BUYER'S AGENT

If you want an agent to work for you, hire one. Although buyer's agents have been arranging commercial property sales for a long time, home buyers traditionally have had no representation in the real estate marketplace. Only recently have such agents become popular among residential buyers. Hiring your own agent to help you find a house and negotiate a deal is often a good idea, especially because buyer's agents can show and bargain for almost any house listed in the community, even those for sale by owners. They cannot, however, show you properties listed for sale by their own real estate companies because that would involve them in a conflict of interest prohibited by law.

Shopping for an Agent

Any licensed real estate agent can represent home buyers. Some agencies specialize in representing buyers instead of sellers. Most of these are located in medium-sized and large cities.

Look for someone with whom you can establish a good relationship, because you might be working together for weeks or months. Important professional qualities to consider are experience, intelligence, integrity, resourcefulness and intuition. Knowledge of the industry, houses and the community are particularly important. Again, the one- or two-office brokerage may well prove to be the best bet; it can offer you personal service and spend more time answering your questions and looking after your needs. Such personal attention can go a long way toward eliminating the anxiety of home buyers caught in the complexities of the real estate marketplace.

The first thing an experienced agent will do is ask questions to find out whether you are qualified to buy the type of house you're looking for. At this point you should also be evaluating the agent. Ask if the agent has a strong background. Talk to others about the agent's record. Find out about the agent's technical know-how, perhaps by talking to a former client. Ask about expertise with contracts, negotiating ability, record of cooperation with other brokers and influence with moneylenders.

The Buyer's Agent Contract

When you hire a buyer's agent, you enter a contract for services. With a fee "up front" or an hourly fee, you pay the agent to find you a house and negotiate a deal for you. You should reasonably expect agents to save you both time and money. If they can't tell you how they'll do this, you may want to look elsewhere. Here are some questions to ask when negotiating your service contract:

• How will the fee be calculated?
• Is there a minimum charge?
• How long will the contract be in force?
• What happens if you find a house on your own?
• How will disputes be resolved?

Most buyer's agents will offer to work for a flat fee. Few will work on commission and, as we've discussed before, if you find one who does, stay away, as this arrangement gives the agent an incentive to sell you a home at the highest possible price. This creates a conflict you will want to avoid.

"FOR SALE BY OWNER"

Some owners choose to sell their houses on their own, without a broker. At first glance, this looks like an automatic saving for the buyer in every case, because no commission has to be paid. But be sure to examine carefully any "discount" and to keep in mind that an owner unwilling to pay a commission to a broker may be just as unwilling to pass savings on to you.

Always remember the overriding truth about buying and selling anything: sellers charge what the market will bear. Although an owner can offer a house for a few thousand dollars less than what the asking price would be if a broker's commission had to be paid, there may be little incentive to pass the savings on to the buyer; many owners prefer to keep it for themselves.

Use this as a bargaining chip when you're the buyer. Suggest to the seller that he or she is already saving a substantial amount by not having to pay a broker's commission and ask for a price reduction that at least splits this amount between you. Find out what the prevailing commission percentage is in your area and reduce the seller's asking price by half of that percentage. You'll probably strike a deal.

PREPARING TO BUY

If you plan to sell your current residence first, it may be best to start advertising it for sale before beginning your search, but make sure you have already done your homework and can begin home hunting immediately. Be sure not to commit yourself to purchasing a new home until the old one is sold. On the other hand, give yourself enough time, and try to sell to a buyer who is willing to wait until you find your new home.

If you find a new home first, you'll be more likely to sell your current one quickly and perhaps too cheaply. Also, unless you can afford to own two homes, you may find yourself in a weak position—offering to buy the home only if you sell yours first—an offer sellers may be reluctant to accept.

The danger of being without a place to live can be avoided by delaying the closing on your existing residence. You can also rent, but until you buy your new home, you'll be sacrificing your income tax deduction of mortgage interest and you will incur the expense of moving, of committing to a lease, and possibly of storage charges.

CHAPTER **6**

LEGAL LIMITS

In your search for a home to buy, you should consider the physical aspects of the property such as garage and storage space and whether the roof is sound. These will be covered in the next chapter. This chapter is concerned with the legal inspection—those rules that could seriously restrict your freedom to use the property you buy in any way you want.

The state, county, city or neighborhood can all legally restrict your right to use your property. Unless you ask the right questions now, you may be in for surprises later.

EASEMENTS AND SHARED USE

Separate elements of what you own, such as the underground mineral rights, can be sold or leased without giving up ownership of the land surface. You can also allow another person limited use of your real estate by granting an *easement*—an interest in real estate that lasts forever, unless otherwise specified, and that allows a specific limited use of a parcel of land.

Easements are granted for a wide range of activities. The most common easements are for streets or public utility lines. Another common easement is for the use of a common driveway to reach the backyards of neighboring houses.

Ask the seller or agent if there are any *formal* easements on the property. If there are, they will show up in the title search (see Chapter 13), but it's better to know about them now and decide beforehand whether you want to buy into the limitations they'll impose on your use of the property. Ask also if any *informal* easements or agreements exist. Sometimes, for example, there is an agreement to allow a neighbor to come onto the property to cut overhanging branches. Sometimes, by custom, neighbors use a path that cuts through the property. Although these informal understandings between neighbors are not always enforceable in court, your awareness of them can make for better relations after you move in.

Existing uses of another's property can be enforced in three ways. The first is through an easement that has developed over time and is all but permanent, such as the use of half of the driveway (a "party driveway") you share with your neighbor.

The second is through "adverse possession," what most of us think of as "squatter's rights." This is a legal doctrine that permits a squatter to hold ownership rights over someone else's piece of property if the squatter meets certain legal requirements set down in your state's case law. Typically, these requirements include open and uncontested use of the property with no attempt to hide for a designated number of years. If the owner makes no protest during that time, the property can be declared owned by the squatter.

The third is through the "party wall" doctrine. A party wall is the shared wall between two properties. Each owner has an equal shared interest in the wall. Each can do as he or she pleases with his or her side of the wall. Most attached city residences have party walls.

ZONING

Zoning laws classify property by the way in which it can be used. They restrict what is otherwise an owner's complete freedom to use property. One of the first things you need to do is match what you want to do against the property's zoning classification. For example, making holiday ornaments for sale at your home or taking in children of working parents during the day may be illegal in a residential-only area.

Some common classifications are "residential only," "single-family dwellings only," "commercial only" and "mixed use." You have no assurance that the present classification won't be changed, but, as a property owner, you'll be warned about it if a change is being contemplated. You will at least have a chance to speak your mind about it at any public hearing or by writing letters to the zoning authority. Zoning changes are often hotly contested, especially in residential areas where rezoning requests are to allow commercial development.

Variances

Even more hotly contested are *variance* requests. These are individual owners' requests to allow special exceptions to zoning restrictions. An example would be a request by someone in a residential-only zone to be allowed to open a dentist's office. Sometimes when such requests are made, a sign is placed in front of the property and a notice is mailed to all owners within a specified distance advising them of a public hearing on the matter. Hotly contested variance requests can tear a neighborhood apart. Check to see if any are pending before you buy.

Zoning is important not only for what you want to do with your property, but also for what your neighbors want to do with theirs. If high-rise apartments are permitted in the neighborhood and you don't want to live next to one, think hard about that choice. Agents, the local recorder of deeds and the city or county zoning office can all tell you how the neighborhood you're interested in is zoned.

RESTRICTIVE COVENANTS

Restrictive covenants are similar to zoning restrictions but are much more specific to each parcel of land. These restrictions are as enforceable as zoning laws.

Such covenants go beyond general zoning restrictions to require that residents perform certain tasks such as mowing their lawns every two weeks, or refrain from doing certain things considered harmful to the community. Some communities ban backyard satellite dishes. Others ban cars in favor of horse-drawn vehicles.

These kinds of covenants are typical in many communities, ranging from large sprawling suburban developments that restrict the type of landscaping to co-op apartments that prohibit installation of fireplaces or hot tubs.

If you are thinking of buying into a condominium or co-op, try to talk to current residents and ask what covenants are in place, whether they are enforced and whether the association's governing board ever acts on requests by members or groups of members to change them. The bylaws of the association should spell out what it takes to amend these rules.

Restrictive covenants can be found in your deed, in the bylaws that govern the association that runs the co-op or condominium, and in resolutions that have been passed by the association. Ask for a compilation of earlier association resolutions, which is not usually provided when you are given the bylaws and other governing documents. Also, look at the minutes from recent board meetings to see what issues the association has been dealing with.

For single-family, detached housing, you will want to contact any local neighborhood association and talk to neighbors. If you don't ask about something, you may not become aware of a restriction on how you can use your new property until you violate it. You may also not know that certain amenities—a pool, for example—are unprotected by any written agreement and may be taken away.

In the past, restrictive covenants were widely used to prevent owners from selling their houses to members of minority groups. Now all such discriminatory covenants are illegal and should be reported to the nearest office of the U.S. Department of Housing and Urban Development (see Appendix II).

DEVELOPMENT PATTERNS

If you are on or near the dividing line between two zoned areas, you will want to know what is permitted in the area next to you. If a huge factory is across an open field from you, it's safe to assume that if the company expands, the open field is likely to become a megawatt electricity generator or a parking lot. Survey the neighborhood. Ask neighbors, agents and merchants about past development trends and known or expected developments in the future. Is the area fairly stable or in transition? Has any developer announced a major project in the vicinity? Is the local government planning to close a school, build a new prison, open a new subway route? As always, a little homework now can save headaches and surprises later.

RED TAPE REQUIREMENTS

What you can and can't do with your house depends a lot on your local, county and state governments. Cities and counties often require permits and inspections for everything from building a sun deck to installing electrical appliances. There are rules about parking cars on the street at night, barking dogs, burning leaves, shoveling snow, trash pickup and size and location of mailboxes. Many rules are for safety—prohibition of portable kerosene heaters, for example. Others can seem to be nuisances you would prefer to avoid.

Although some regulations may seem trivial, all of them can be enforced by fines. The best way to learn what they are in your area is from the state, county and local offices of licensing, regulatory affairs and public works. Also check with any property owners' associations, tax districts, club management and other organizations by whose rules you will be governed should you purchase a particular property. Also ask your prospective neighbors what you have to do for permission to add an extension to your house, build a patio or install central air-conditioning.

CONSUMER PROTECTION

By now you may feel you're being thrown to the wolves. You've been warned that the broker may sound friendly but has interests that are contrary to your own. You've been warned that the seller's first objective is collecting a high price. And you've been warned about a host of rules, restrictions and red tape. It's all true, and you do have to be careful, but here comes the good part: it's not a jungle out there. Laws have been adopted to protect real estate buyers from certain unethical practices, and the number of such laws increases each year. There are also business standards that are enforced by professional associations.

A Code of Ethics

The National Association of Realtors has adopted a code of conduct for realtors. You can get a copy by writing to the association at 430 North Michigan Ave., Chicago, IL 60611. The code applies only to brokers and agents who are members of the association, however. Violation of the code does not necessarily lead to legal action, but it could result in disciplinary action after a proceeding. All violations should be reported to the association. Among other things, the code provides for:

Fairness   Realtors must protect and promote the interests of clients. In doing this, they are obligated to treat fairly all parties to the transaction, including the buyer.

Misrepresentation   Realtors must not exaggerate, misrepresent or hide pertinent facts.

Investigation   Realtors must discover all adverse facts a reasonably competent investigation would disclose. Agents are not, however, required to conduct their own inspections of the houses they sell and disclose to prospective buyers all defects they find.

Full Disclosure   If a realtor receives compensation from more than one party to a transaction, all parties must be informed of it. They also must disclose to buyers that they work for the seller.

Conflict of Interest   Realtors are forbidden to provide professional services involving a property in which they have a present or contemplated interest unless full disclosure is made.

Written Notification   All financial obligations and commitments regarding real estate must be in writing that expresses the exact agreement of the parties.

Unauthorized Practice of Law   The code forbids realtors from engaging in the unauthorized practice of law (UPL). Realtors are obligated instead to recommend that legal counsel be obtained. This limitation is also included in bar association rules and is discussed in Chapter 8.

Court Protection

Breach of Contract   Because the purchase of a home is a contract, as a buyer you can sue the seller if you find intentional misrepresentations that caused a breach of that contract. You'll probably also be able to sue the seller's broker if he or she participated in any deceit—lying about the kind of tile in the kitchen, providing a false set of co-op or condo bylaws that omits certain provisions, misrepresenting the age of appliances, and so on. Any breach of the contract that is substantial can be the basis for a lawsuit.

Condominium Development Problems   In some areas a significant history of fraud and misrepresentation has been developing in the sale of new condominiums. Unscrupulous developers and sales representatives have lured buyers into deals with sophisticated sales pitches and then sold them defective units or failed to make proper disclosures.

States have responded with laws that require certain written disclosures up front and give consumers redress for violations. To find out more about special protection for condominium purchasers in your state and what you should expect, call your state office of consumer protection and ask for the office that handles condominium sales.

Court battles over these issues are both common and messy. They also cover a wide array of abuses. Sometimes the developer has fled the state or declared bankruptcy and gone out of business. Other developers have signed contracts to sell units but with no deadline for the sale and then delayed completing construction until the buyer backed out, kept the buyer's deposit and sold the unit to another buyer at an inflation-increased price. Lawsuits over condo construction defects are also common.

Your best bet is to check up on the developer and talk to

other owners, especially in areas where many condominium developments are being built. Remember that fraud flourishes and hides best where business is booming.

Although your right to file a lawsuit is secure, doing so is difficult and expensive. If you believe you are the victim of developer fraud, try to band with others similarly situated and hire legal counsel to work for all of you. Combining resources can make your lawsuit less a drain on your budget and emotions.

Discrimination   Under the federal fair housing laws, it is illegal to discriminate because of race, sex, color or national origin. The realtors' code of ethics requires the same. Some local and state laws have even stricter standards. For instance, in the District of Columbia it is illegal to discriminate in housing based on any of sixteen different characteristics, including age, marital status and political affiliation.

Certain cities have their own laws: for instance, New York forbids discrimination on the basis of sexual orientation or the presence of children. You can find out on which bases discrimination is forbidden by calling your state or local office of human rights. They may also have pamphlets or other consumer information on this subject.

Discrimination is sometimes hard to detect. Examples of how it is practiced include:

- You're told the home is sold when it is not.
- You're told there are competing offers.
- You are asked to leave your telephone number, and if the first three digits can be traced to a minority residential area, no one calls you back.
- You're told the seller has decided not to sell or has raised the price.
- The broker says there's nothing available in your price range and refuses to show you the listing of homes for sale.

- No one is available to show you the home, you can't get an appointment or the agent cancels an appointment without explanation.
- You're told the house isn't what you want, is too expensive or isn't desirable.

If you think you've been the victim of discrimination, you have several options. You can file a civil lawsuit, complain to the area office of human rights or to the office that handles discrimination complaints, contact the U.S. Department of Housing and Urban Development (see Appendix II) or contact the National Association of Realtors. Your remedies will vary depending on how you proceed.

A civil lawsuit can result in your receiving damages. A complaint to the National Association of Realtors will not. Depending on your state's human rights law, you may be able to receive damages from the administrative agency if you prove discrimination. All of these options, however, are time-consuming, and inconvenient and can be expensive. Many of the state and local offices of human rights have caseworkers who will work with you to file a charge. In addition, depending on the type of discrimination, there are national and state organizations that may be able to help, such as Legal Counsel for the Elderly, the National Association for the Advancement of Colored People and the National Organization for Women. Even though they can't enter the case directly, groups such as these should be able to provide information and referrals.

Reforming the Profession

As you have seen, you do have recourse if you think you have been unfairly treated as a buyer of real estate. Nevertheless, it is important that you be cautious. You are making a major investment of money that will probably require a major change in your family life. Protect yourself by going to reputable brokers, by getting written assurances along the way, by consulting the professional watchdog organizations and government agencies and reading as much consumer information as you can find. Bear in mind that although not everyone is "out to get you," you are, in the end, your own best advocate.

CHAPTER 7

INSPECTIONS

After you've found one or two homes you're interested in, it's time to learn what they're worth. This chapter tells you some of the things to look for as well as how to protect yourself against current and future problems.

THE SHOWING

Usually several inspections are made. First is a showing by the owner or broker. As mentioned earlier, this can be an open house for all comers or an individual showing with just you and a broker. If the home is for sale by its owner, the owner will probably show you around. No matter how it's done, the primary purpose is the sales pitch—an orchestrated attempt to get you to see all the positive things being offered.

At this early stage in the house-buying process, you need not be too concerned about detailed structural characteristics. That comes later. For now, listen to the sales pitch and ask yourself how many of your requirements—your musts, options and dreams—will be satisfied by this home. Is there central air-conditioning? Is the home heated by gas, oil or electricity? How high are the winter fuel bills? What is the neighborhood's zoning classification? Is street parking restricted? What school services the neighborhood? What is the general appearance of the other homes in the area?

Feel free to open doors and go places the agent isn't showing you. People who are having their house shown should have prepared for it. They should expect you to snoop around. If they don't want you to, be suspicious.

Try not to leave the house until you have a good idea of whether you want to follow up on it. You'll have a chance later to do a more thorough inspection. Now is the time to decide whether the house is a definite "no" or a definite prospect.

THE DETAILED INSPECTION

Sometime before closing, you need a detailed inspection of the home. You should also have the property *appraised* to make sure the asking price is in the right range. Many buyers skip these important steps because the lender, usually a bank, will also inspect, appraise and survey the property. The lender's inspection and appraisal, however, don't protect *you,* because the law doesn't require them to be comprehensive.

Several good guides and manuals are available that itemize what you should look for when you inspect the house (see the bibliography, Appendix IV). They will alert you to where and how to look, and in some cases how to interpret what you find.

If you're buying a home that is more than ten years old and expect to live in it for several years, you should consider hiring a professional inspector or at least consulting with someone whose judgment you trust, who has inspected homes in the past and knows what to look for. If, however, you decide to make your own inspection, consult the checklist in Appendix I as well as books in the bibliography.

Professional Inspectors   A professional inspector can be an architect, engineer, carpenter, contractor or building consultant, but avoid using someone who might benefit from work you expect to contract for later. Companies that do this work are called building or home inspection services. Listings can be found in your telephone book, or you can get referrals from the broker or from friends who have used services in the past. Be cautious about proceeding blindly without references: anyone who wants to do so can advertise as an inspector. Ask for recommendations and check qualifications and professional affiliations. Members of the American Society of Home Inspectors, for example, must pass a comprehensive entrance examination, agree to participate in continuing education classes and either complete 1,000 paid house inspections or meet additional education requirements and complete 400 paid inspections.

The inspection will usually take one to two hours. If you are buying an older home or one that is being bought "as is," the inspection may take as long as five or six hours. Standard charges range from $100 to $300, almost always paid by the buyer. Many inspectors encourage buyers to go through the home with them. You should do this and take notes. Many of the inspection services routinely include in their price a written report and a binder that describes the home's systems. But you should also ask for a written report on major structural elements:

- The capacity of the heating and cooling systems in relation to the size of the house
- The age of the systems and their normal life expectancy
- The condition and adequacy of the electrical wiring and plumbing
- Notes on appliances and water heater
- Repairs and additions that may be needed soon
- The condition of the basement, crawl spaces and attic,

with attention to moisture, ventilation, insulation and construction
• The condition of the roof, gutters, downspouts, drainage, siding, caulking and paint, and the extent of impending structural repairs

You need not bother too much with an inspection for termites. Most home purchase contracts require the seller to order and pay for that.

Inspections for Radon, Asbestos, Lead and Chemicals These are services that you may want to inquire about, especially if the locale has a history of this or the property is near a chemical plant. These inspections usually cost $40 to $200 and sometimes take additional time. For instance, a test for radon, a carcinogen, can be done in two days but may also involve a test that takes thirty days.

Before signing for these additional inspections, ask the companies you're considering hiring whether they have done homes in the area and whether they have found traces of any of the agents mentioned above. You can also call your state's environmental protection office and see if your community has any history of these problems. If both of these inquiries produces a "no" answer, you probably do not need to incur the extra expense.

Many buyers include an "inspection contingency" clause in their contract. This gives them the right to withdraw from the contract if the inspection reveals defects (page 70).

After the inspection you will have a specified number of days to negotiate with the seller about whatever was revealed that you want fixed before you remove the "inspection contingency." A limit of three to seven days is typical. Many buyers total what they think making the repairs will cost and present this figure to the seller. Often, part of the inspection includes estimates of repair costs. A seller who does not want to make the repairs may simply reduce the asking price by that amount if it's reasonable.

HOMEOWNERS WARRANTY (HOW)

If the house you want to buy is less than ten years old, it may be covered by a Homeowners Warranty (HOW), a warranty from a private insurance company that gives new houses ten years of protection against faulty construction. The warranty is backed by insurance and remains with the house if it is sold within the first ten years. Subsequent purchasers within ten years of building are covered. The policy transfers automatically.

If a builder refuses to correct mistakes, insurance covers the repairs. A built-in dispute-settling process determines the outcome when the buyer and builder disagree. This allows you to avoid costly, long, difficult litigation if problems arise.

The builder pays a fee for the HOW policy that is usually passed along to the buyer as part of the selling price. A buyer of a $100,000 house, for example, can expect that $200 to $500 of that price is for the HOW coverage.

During the first year, HOW builders guarantee their new houses are free of defective work and materials, major structural defects, and flaws in the electrical, plumbing, heating, cooling, ventilation and mechanical systems. They guarantee the same items during the second year of the policy, but don't guarantee the work and materials. In the remaining eight years of HOW protection, the house is insured only against major structural defects.

Ask about HOW protection if you are buying a home less than ten years old. Many builders selling new homes use the HOW as a promotional device, so expect a strong sales pitch and to be told that the builder is paying for it for you. If you are the second or subsequent buyer, ask about the HOW and get a copy. More likely than not, if a policy exists, you will be given a copy.

OTHER NEW-HOME WARRANTIES

Some builders choose not to purchase HOW coverage, and some offer warranty programs of their own. It is expected that during the next few years, more builders will decide to offer their own warranty programs and other national and local programs will begin competing with HOW.

In evaluating a warranty, check first with your state insurance commissioner's office. Ask whether that office has any information on the company offering the coverage. A history of complaints against the company should serve as a warning. Also make sure the policy requires arbitration of disputes because without it the policy is a good-faith promise rather than a true warranty.

USED-HOME WARRANTIES

If you're thinking of buying a used home, be sure to have a careful inspection. You can purchase insurance that protects you from defects not revealed during an inspection. Usually, the cost is about one-tenth of one percent of the home's purchase price and carries a low deductible, typically a few hundred dollars. Policies are offered for one year and are not available after that without a new buyer and new inspection.

A warranty service or insurance doesn't tell you whether a house is well built, and it won't tell you if the house is underwired or if the plumbing is badly corroded. All that is assured by the typical warranty is that specified mechanical equipment will remain operating for a year after you buy the house.

The buyer usually buys the warranty and is responsible for paying a deductible if anything goes wrong during the warranty period. And remember, the warranty is not in any sense an assurance that the equipment is in good condition. In fact, rarely do any of the major companies that offer warranty services inspect the properties they cover.

If you want to purchase this policy, call companies in your area and ask if they require an inspection and which inspection services are acceptable to them. Use one of those companies.

WHEN TO INSPECT

Don't spend money and time on an inspection and appraisal unless you're prepared to buy the property if everything checks out. If you are prepared to buy, then by all means inspect the property. The information you get could help significantly during price negotiations.

When you make an offer to buy a house, do it in writing and include a statement that gives you enough time to have the property inspected and an "out" if the property doesn't pass muster. Normally you won't be given much time because sellers and brokers are reluctant to take the property off the market for long. Also, they worry that a buyer with second thoughts can use the inspection report to get out of the deal.

Chapter 8 discusses purchase contracts that protect your interests. At this point you need know only that unless your preliminary contract makes the sale contingent on a satisfactory inspection of the house, you will *not* be protected. Inspections should satisfy you and you should release the contingency only when they do.

If you're buying a new property, many state laws protect you and you can purchase HOW coverage. Just to be sure, add a clause to your contract requiring the builder to comply with all state, local and county regulations.

THE APPRAISAL

Though your lender will do an appraisal after you apply for a loan, you may want one for yourself now. Before you hire a professional appraiser, you should understand what determines the true value of a house. A house is not valued for its carpeting or wallpaper, the owner's furnishings or appliances, fancy lighting or bathroom fixtures, paint colors, equipment you don't want or need, or the sentiments of the present owner.

True value is determined by the amount of land and landscaping; the size and number of rooms and bathrooms; the size of the kitchen and its storage space; the size and condition of the basement, attic and screened-in porches; the quality of construction; whether electrical, plumbing, heating and cooling systems are new or in good repair; energy-saving features such as storm windows, insulation and heat pumps; new roof, gutters and siding; and the convenience and value of the location.

Ask the agent selling the house to show you a recent market analysis of the property, but recognize that it may be unrealistically favorable to the seller. Try to determine whether the person who did the analysis was a trained, objective specialist. If you're satisfied that the house is priced fairly and in line with what similar properties have sold for recently, you probably can safely dispense with an independent appraisal. However, if you discover something unusual, by all means have your own appraisal done. Warning signals to watch for include property that has been on the market a long time, property that has an expensive new addition, and property that is much less developed than its neighbors.

For your appraisal, you can hire a disinterested real estate broker or a professional appraiser. Remember that the institution that loans you the money to buy your house will want an appraisal too, so if you can get the lender to approve of your appraiser, it could eliminate the need for and cost of a second appraisal.

These professional appraiser organizations require training and an internship:

- The American Institute of Real Estate Appraisers, 430 N. Michigan Ave, Chicago, IL 60611
- The Society of Real Estate Appraisers, 645 N. Michigan Ave., Chicago, IL 60611

It is important to hire an appraiser who knows the community. Look for a company that has good local ties and connections.

Appraisals vary, so before you hire an appraiser explain exactly why you want an appraisal and ask what it will cost. Depending where you live, you can pay anywhere from $150 to $350. The appraisal should include a list of *limiting conditions,* those aspects of a house that reduce its value: for example, an old roof or a cracked foundation. It should also include pictures of the house and street, a map locating the site and, possibly, a floor plan.

THE LENDER'S ROLE

Your lender is sure to inspect and appraise the home before making you a loan. The inspection and appraisal determine only whether the lender will be able to sell the property and get back the amount invested if you fail to make your payments. Beyond that, the lender's interest goes only far enough to assure that the house is structurally sound enough that you won't go bankrupt repairing it and have to default on the loan. You will want your own inspection to be so comprehensive that it reveals all defects that will need repair, not only the major ones.

LET THE BUYER BEWARE

The overriding motto for property buyers used to be "let the buyer beware." Now more than half of the states have enacted laws that impose on builders an "implied warranty of fitness or quality" in work and materials. The enactment of such laws in so many states reflects a growing tendency by government to protect home buyers from defects in home building. However, most states that have such implied warranties protect only first-time buyers, not resale purchasers. Few states give resale purchasers the same protection they give first-time buyers. To find out whether your state has a law creating an implied warranty of fitness or quality, look in your state code under the section on property or real estate or call your state department of housing.

The rule to follow is still simple: whatever you're buying, the more warranties you can get in writing, the better. The next chapter covers some warranties you should consider putting in your purchase contract.

THE CONTRACT

Once you have found the home you want, it's time to negotiate a contract with the owner. This contract will control everything about the property transfer, including the financing, so by now you should also be well along in your search for a loan. (Chapter 9 discusses financing in detail.)

Getting a purchase contract signed and in force involves five steps:

- *The offer to buy.* The first step is your written offer to purchase. It includes the price you are willing to pay and any other conditions you want to impose and is backed by a deposit of a check, called *earnest money.* Many people make the initial offer in writing, using a prewritten contract form; then, when the deal goes through, the same piece of paper serves as the final contract.
- *The counteroffer.* The seller now accepts your price or makes a counteroffer, also in writing. When many offers and counteroffers are made, the parties may put only the final, agreed-upon price and other conditions on the contract form, or write the terms into a separate agreement.
- *The binder agreement (or tentative contract).* When you and the seller agree on the price, you both sign an "agreement to agree," known as the *binder* or preliminary contract. It formalizes the acceptance of a price and the promise to continue negotiating.
- *Purchase negotiation.* All the terms of the purchase—date,

type of financing, inspections, condition of the title and property and all other details—now have to be negotiated in good faith.

- *The final contract.* The final step is the signing of the final purchase contract. This contract is what your negotiating produces. It lists every aspect and term of the deal. Contracts for the sale of real estate must be in writing to be enforceable.

THE OFFER

To get the ball rolling, you, as the buyer, make an offer. All serious offers should be in writing and signed by you or your agent. You should make your offer through the seller's broker, if the seller has one. In fact, if an agent or broker is involved, you may not meet the seller until the closing. Include a time limit for a response, but don't allow too long—a few days, perhaps three to four in a competitive market—should be enough. The more time you allow the seller to scout for other offers, the more likely it is that yours will be topped.

State in your written offer that you are prepared to back it up with cash—called earnest money. This is money you are ready to hand over as soon as your offer is accepted. Its purpose is to demonstrate your seriousness. It is not the down payment. Even on a very large, expensive house, $1,000–$5,000 is quite routine. Whether your earnest money is refundable if the deal falls through is a matter for negotiation. You may want to state in your initial offer that your earnest money is to be refunded if you can't strike a deal.

THE COUNTEROFFER

The seller either accepts your price and preliminary terms or makes a counterproposal. That counteroffer may be to accept your price but leave all other matters to negotiation. Alternatively, the seller might ask a higher price but agree to your other conditions, such as refunding your deposit if the deal falls through. You can agree to disagree and go shopping for another home to buy, you can make another offer or you can agree to the seller's terms. To go forward with negotiations, sooner or later you'll have to agree at least to a price. When you do, it's time to sign the binder agreement.

THE BINDER AGREEMENT OR TENTATIVE CONTRACT

The binder is your agreement to agree, but despite its name, it is not fully binding. It simply demonstrates your desire to go forward and discuss the details of the contract. It does, however, bind both sides to a price and forbids the seller from signing a contract with someone else. The seller may, however, continue to accept "backup" contracts in the event your negotiations fall through. You are now into full scale negotiation. Again, the terms you negotiate are usually preprinted directly on a standard-form contract; provisions you or the seller want that are not already printed on the form can be added in an addendum or rider.

NEGOTIATING THE PURCHASE

Once the binder is signed by both sides and the earnest money is handed over, the seller must negotiate in good faith. This doesn't mean you, the buyer, can't walk away from the deal. It means that if you do walk away from it, you may lose your earnest money unless provisions were made in advance about its refund. This is true on both sides. If negotiations reach stalemate, you can both walk away from the deal. If the seller is the one who refuses to negotiate further, you can and should demand a refund of your earnest money.

Although most agents and sellers use standard-form real estate contracts, there's room for negotiation on every provision, especially if you are persistent, informed and reasonable. Some of the terms to watch for and insist upon in your contract are discussed later in this chapter, but every property is unique. In addition to the items discussed here, you should also develop your own conditions for going through with the deal. You will have to include these in your initial offer.

Contingencies

Buyers typically put four standard "contingencies" in their contracts that are recognized throughout the industry. It's important to note that any contingency will weaken your position relative to a competing buyer's offer that has fewer strings attached, but these four are the most common and you should consider them:

- Making your offer contingent on an inspection of the premises that is suitable to you
- Making your offer contingent on your reading the condominium or co-op bylaws and budgets
- Making your offer contingent on the sale of your existing residence
- Making your offer contingent on obtaining financing

Needless to say, the last two can be a problem to the seller who will have no control over them. In many instances the seller will not want to take the chance that you won't be able to sell your home or get financing. One way to reduce the seller's concern over such contingencies is by putting a deadline on each or demonstrating that there will be no problem, such as by showing you already have offers to buy your existing residence or agreeing to get a "preapproval" letter from a loan officer. You usually can get a loan preapproval with one interview; although it doesn't bind the lender, it is recognized as assurance that you will get financing if all your information is confirmed.

The Price

Think long and hard about the price you will offer. Many people rely on suggestions from those in real estate and in other guides and offer 85% to 90% of the asking price. This is no hard and fast formula, however, and you should consider a number of things before settling on an offer. For instance, consider:

- How long has the property been on the market?
- How many condo or co-op units in the same building or houses on the same street are for sale and competing with this one?
- What is the market like? In broker's lingo, is it "soft"? Are interest rates so high that people aren't buying? Are you entering the holiday season, when sales are really slow? A slow market means you may not have a lot of competition. A fast market has lots of buyers competing with each other and could mean your offer should be *higher* than the asking price.
- How badly do you want the place? Many people make low offers and then learn that if they had offered $1,000 more they would have succeeded. Weigh your desire for the home against your desire to get a good deal.
- What else can you offer the seller to sweeten the deal or to make you more attractive and less risky than the next buyer? Are you offering a large down payment, thereby reducing the risk you'll be turned down for a loan? Can you offer to pay a large chunk of the closing costs up front?
- Does the seller have to unload the home, for example because a divorce is in progress or the seller is under pressure to close the deal on another home?

In your negotiations with the seller or the agent, keep everything businesslike and avoid showing any emotion about your interest or enthusiasm for the property. Good agents will play on these emotions. Likewise, the more you can find out about the property and seller's situation, the better you will be at making offers and setting terms. If you want to talk directly to the seller, insist on it. Brokers frown on this practice, but it is done. The broker needs you to make the sale and has an interest in pleasing you. Remember that the more time a particular broker "invests" in you, the more he or she stands to lose if the deal falls through.

Finally, be forceful but not stubborn. Depending on the market and the availability of other potential buyers, the seller may bend, but you also run the risk of breaking the deal. Try to get an indication from the broker of how far you can push the seller. All the information you collected about the seller and property will be helpful in determining how to negotiate.

Negotiating the purchase of real estate is one area in which reading general materials can be especially helpful. Check the bibliography (Appendix IV) for sources.

THE FINAL CONTRACT

The final purchase contract contains an exchange of promises. The seller promises to deliver to you a good and marketable title along with the deed, and you promise to pay a specified sum in cash. The contract binds both the buyer and seller to go through with the deal on mutually agreed-upon terms. It can also give the buyer time to arrange a mortgage, to make sure there are no defects in the seller's title to the property and to arrange title insurance.

A final real estate contract is generally assumed to be all-inclusive. Everything of importance should be written into it. Your contract should include the purchase price, down payment, a description of the property and a list of other items being sold with the house. It should specify how the ownership is to be transferred to you, the method of payment, the financing arrangement, the amount of the deposit, the conditions under which you or the seller can void the contract, any defects in the property or title, the settlement date and how financing will be arranged.

Some people ask a lawyer to review their contract. By all means, if it has provisions you don't understand, ask someone, possibly a lawyer, to interpret it. However, you probably don't need to pay a lawyer to look after your interests, especially if you are already represented by a "buyer's broker" or have been through the process before. (See page 83 if you decide to use a lawyer.)

The following paragraphs describe the most important protections you need to negotiate and write into your contract.

Getting Back Your Deposit   When you put down a deposit (earnest money), you assure the seller that you plan to go through with the deal. Make sure, however, that your purchase depends on whatever developments might force you to cancel the deal—the contingencies—and build in the obligation to return your money if these points cannot be resolved.

Nonfixtures   Anything that isn't more or less attached to the land is not automatically included in the property transfer. Those things that are permanently attached to the house—a fireplace, for instance—are deemed fixtures and are transferred automatically with the sale. If you want possession of anything that is in the house but may not be a fixture, write it into the contract. Ask about anything you're unsure of. For instance, bookcases, cabinets, wall units that look built in, chandeliers, above-ground swimming pools, picnic and outdoor furniture, built-in barbecue grills, and stoves, refrigerators and other appliances. A good time to get all this nailed down is during the inspection. Then write it into the contract.

Settlement Costs   In the negotiation of the contract, certain of the closing costs can be assigned to the parties. Others are often determined by local custom and aren't put into the contract. You can save money by figuring the closing costs ahead of time and including them in the contract as part of the purchase price. That way they will be covered by your loan. Chapter 13 discusses the closing in greater detail and includes a comprehensive list of common closing costs.

Contingencies   Write all your contingencies into the contract: inspection, financing, sale of your existing residence, review of the condo or co-op association bylaws.

Warranties   If you have agreed to accept the property with any defects, have them listed specifically. Include any warranties that "run" with the property such as the HOW purchased by the builder for any homes less than ten years old, as well as other builder warranties. Also, if other warranties are available from recent renovations or repairs, it's a good idea to include them.

Closing Date   Require the seller to pay you rent if the home isn't vacated and available to you by the agreed-upon date. This is called a *rent-back* clause.

STANDARD-FORM CONTRACTS

In almost all cases, you will be offered a standard real estate contract, a "complete" document with blank spaces for provisions such as a description of the property and other matters unique to a specific property. Matters you want included should be discussed *before* signing, not conceded merely because they were not contained in the standard form.

Because everything in a real estate contract is open to

negotiation, every contract is unique. The standard "fill-in-the-blanks" form real estate professionals use should be modified to fit your purchase. You will have to add important provisions, delete others, modify still others.

It's important enough to repeat: *nothing about a real estate deal is enforceable unless it is in writing and in the contract.* Any changes you make to the standard form must be initialed by both you and the seller. Even when standard forms have no room to add words, you are free to insist that provisions be crossed out and that additional provisions be included on a separate page as a rider or addendum.

The standard contract used in various forms all over the country is by no means a plain-language document. When you are handed one, take the time to read it carefully, line by line, and *make sure you understand every clause.* Don't be rushed. Words like "warrants," "guarantees" and "marketable" all have specific meanings. (Most of the terms you're likely to see are included in the glossary, Appendix III.) Custom in your area can also affect how certain language in the contract is interpreted. A plain-language contract is preferable and you certainly should ask for one, but don't feel you have failed if you're told to accept the standard contract or look elsewhere. Our society is still far from the day when laws require that all contracts be written in language that can be understood without specialized training or education.

You can get a sample standard-form contract from a broker. If you familiarize yourself with it beforehand, you are less likely to be intimidated or deceived when your seller's agent hands you a contract.

TAKE YOUR TIME

Don't be rushed into signing anything you are unsure about. Ask questions, voice doubts, read materials, inspect again. Talk to professionals. Talk to others who have bought houses recently. Educate yourself by reading as much as you can and ask intelligent questions. Doing your homework is always the best way to become a confident and informed buyer.

LAWYERS' HELP

Because the contract you're offered probably will not be written in plain English, it's prudent to hire a professional to review the terms and make sure they protect your rights. You might be able to find an agent to do this for you. If not—and many agents won't do it for fear of prosecution for unauthorized practice of law (UPL)—your other option is to hire a lawyer. An experienced real estate lawyer should be available for such work at an hourly fee or a flat fee. Prices will vary in different parts of the country, so make a few phone calls to get an idea of what local real estate lawyers charge.

Decide also what role you want the lawyer to fill. You and the seller may want to share a lawyer who will act only as the neutral closing agent and prepare all the papers. If so, you will split the cost and the lawyer will not represent either of you. On the other hand, you can hire a lawyer to protect your rights by reviewing and interpreting the contract, suggesting language, setting up the title searches, preparing the deed and attending the closing with you.

A lawyer won't protect you against every risk, however. You must recognize the distinction between the practical risks every buyer takes and the legal risks a lawyer can explain and help you avoid.

For example, it is up to *you* to make sure the property you're buying is solid land and not a landfill dump that has been landscaped; that it is not in a flood plain; and that the price is right. Once you have advised your lawyer of the practical problems you've discovered, it is up to the lawyer to draft the legal protections to cover them. This doesn't mean your lawyer can't point out practical as well as legal risks, but if he or she does so, you are getting more than legal service. Following are some legal services you can expect from a lawyer's preparation or review of your contract:

Consequences of Breach of Contract   Often a buyer and seller agree upon the performance required of each side but fail to discuss or agree on what happens if one party fails to meet the obligations of the contract. It's always better to plan for all contingencies and decide ahead of time how problems will be handled.

Omissions   Unless you have considerable experience in this area or have done your homework well, you probably won't know whether your contract covers all the necessary points.

Future Effects   Some provisions of a purchase contract may have far-reaching effects, especially when variables like zoning regulations are involved.

Validity   The most important service a lawyer can provide is to assure that the contract is a legally enforceable, binding agreement. This often can depend on including special key phrases unique to the real estate industry.

Negotiation   The difference between negotiating a deal yourself and having an attorney, agent or someone else do it for you is the time the latter allows you to reflect on proposals *before* making a legal commitment to them. When you speak for yourself, you are legally binding yourself unless you state explicitly that you are not. When your agent or attorney negotiates, he or she can allow time to consult with you before responding to the seller. This lets you consider all aspects of an offer without having to make on-the-spot decisions.

Also, if the seller fails to live up to the contract, a negotiator can explore remedies for you better than you can yourself, because friction is less likely when a third, uninvolved person discusses such matters. A negotiator, whether an attorney or not, is paid by you to protect your interest, as a result, a seller is unlikely to question your representative's motives.

AGENTS AND UPL

Remember that if you can find one, you can hire an agent to negotiate for you and advise you about contract provisions. In many places, it is even customary for agents to draw up the contract using standard forms.

Such activity, however, can be restricted by rules that prohibit the unauthorized practice of law (UPL). In many places, nonlawyer brokers and agents cannot write contracts or provide legal advice without running afoul of such laws and facing the risk of prosecution by state bar associations. This has little or nothing to do with the brokers' or agents' abilities. Experienced brokers and agents can describe and advise you about standard real estate contract clauses easily as well as lawyers can, and usually describe them in understandable language. Rather, it is a question of being allowed to compete with lawyers, who provide such routine services for a living.

The problem isn't really yours. It is the broker's or agent's and the organized bar's. You need only be aware of it. If you find experienced brokers or agents willing to provide such services, by all means feel free to use them. You may be able to save a considerable amount of money.

CHAPTER 9

THE MORTGAGE

Few people can afford to buy a home without borrowing some of the money. A working knowledge of mortgages, lenders and how interest rates work is not only helpful, it's essential if you are to avoid being "taken." The uninformed enter the world of financing at their own peril.

Your search for financing should have begun when you decided to start shopping for a home to buy. Given the size and diversity of the modern loan market, you'll need plenty of time to explore the choices of loans and lending institutions available to you.

WHAT IS A MORTGAGE?

When most people speak of home mortgages, they generally are referring to the types of loans that are available to home buyers. A mortgage is *not* a loan. It is the formal document that you, the home buyer, sign pledging your property as security that you will pay off the loan you made to buy it.

In the western United States and in a few areas in the east, a slightly different formal pledge is used. It is called a *deed of trust.* Its only distinguishing characteristic is that it makes it easier for the lender to *foreclose*—the process by which you lose your home if you fail to make your payments on the loan. Otherwise, "mortgage" and "deed of trust" mean the same thing.

MORTGAGE COSTS

The costs of getting a mortgage loan vary, but you can plan on paying some or most of the following:

Points or Discount Points   The lender charges a fee, called *points,* for making the loan. Each point is equal to 1% of the loan amount. It is paid at the closing by the buyer, by the seller, or by both, depending on local custom and, more importantly, on the terms of the contract you negotiated.

The points are prepaid interest to the lender to increase the amount of money the lender takes in initially and to cover the lender's costs of making the loan. The points are interest you would otherwise have to pay later; instead you pay it now, up front. The commitment fee, origination fee (see below) and other service charges may all be included under the umbrella of points, depending on how the lender structures them and local custom.

Loans are offered by lenders for a combination of interest and "up-front" points. Usually you can get a lower interest rate by paying extra points. For example, you may be able to choose a loan at 10% interest plus 4 points, one at 10.5% interest plus 3 points or one at 11% interest plus 2 points. If you have enough cash to pay the higher points at the closing, you can save some interest in later mortgage payments.

If you can get the seller to pay at least some of the points, you'll be even better off, because your seller will be providing some of the up-front cash that lets you choose the lowest-interest-rate loan. Splitting the points between buyer and seller is the custom in some places, so it's worth trying. Ask the seller to pay half the points up to two; this will give you the option of choosing a low-interest loan that requires as much as four points and still only pay two points yourself.

Loan Origination Fee   You'll pay this fee for the administrative cost of processing your application for a loan. It usually is a small amount (1%) of the total you're asking for. It is paid at the closing. On a loan of $100,000, the typical origination fee would be $1,000. It may be included as points.

Commitment Fee   This fee is also paid to the lender. As soon as you decide to accept the lender's financing, it is paid to assure that you will go through with the deal. It usually amounts to 1% of the loan amount. Again, it may be included as part of the points.

Down Payment   This is paid at the closing. It can range from 5% to 20% of the purchase price, but few loans are made for less than 10%. However, a loan can usually be obtained with as small a down payment as 5% under some special government programs. (There are even programs requiring nothing down.) Some states offer guaranteed low-interest loans to first-time home buyers with low down payments. Typically, these are granted according to strict financial-need guidelines. New York, New Jersey, Connecticut and Wisconsin have sponsored such programs. Ask about their availability of any lender that offers home mortgages in your area.

Interest   This is the most important cost you have to consider. Lenders charge interest for the use of their money. This is their primary source of income and your biggest expense. Incurring a loan of $90,000, payable over thirty years at 11% fixed interest, will mean you pay $857.09 every month. If you don't prepay any part of it, you will have paid $308,553.40 by the time you are finished paying off the loan.

Banks set their rates based on the *discount* rate charged to them by the Federal Reserve Board and the *prime* rate. The prime rate is the rate banks charge their "best" customers—usually major corporations. Your rate will be a little higher. Because rates fluctuate and are rarely predictable, lenders offer *adjustable-* or *variable-rate* mortgages, which permit the rate to change during the course of your mortgage.

THE EVER-CHANGING MARKETPLACE

The most difficult part about home buying is finding the right lender and negotiating the right loan. Many good sources of financing information are available. You should look at more than one or two. You will find some recommendations in the bibliography, Appendix IV.

In recent years, the risk caused by fluctuating interest rates has been shifted from lenders to borrowers. Under certain circumstances it may be harder to find loans with fixed interest rates, so that ownership of real estate is no longer a protection against high interest rates and therefore against inflation. When you have an adjustable- or variable-rate mortgage, you can expect to pay higher interest on your loan when inflation drives interest rates up. The net result to you is a higher mortgage payment: your home is costing you more.

When interest rates stabilize, lenders do show signs of going back to fixed interest rates. Nevertheless, fixed-rate loans do not dominate the home market the way they once did. They cannot be counted upon.

Many adjustable- or variable-rate loans offer low initial interest rates, fewer fees in advance and a better payment schedule. In addition, fixed-rate loans now come in terms of fifteen or thirty years. In general, home buyers have more choice and are able to find more finely tuned responses to their borrowing needs in the marketplace.

As a shopper, you will want to consider what lending format is best for you. In particular, you want to consider:

Fixed or Fluctuating?   A fixed rate assures that you'll know what you'll pay regardless what happens to the economy and interest rates. If rates are low, shop for a low-interest fixed rate. If rates are high, consider a fluctuating rate with the knowledge that it will probably go down sometime during the life of the loan and you won't be locked into a high fixed rate.

Also, be wary of low initial interest rates that are sometimes offered to get you to accept a variable-rate loan as an incentive. For instance, you're probably better off with a fixed rate of 10% instead of a loan with a fluctuating rate that starts at 7% for the first two years. If, however, the variable-rate loan can go up by only one percentage point each year and you plan to move in five years, you'll probably pay less interest over that five-year span with the variable-rate loan.

The Rate of Interest and Points   Every additional percentage point you're charged will add thousands of dollars to your total payment, so even if you've decided on a fixed rate, shop for the lowest one possible. Compare lenders and combinations of interest rates and points to get the best deal. A good place to start is the weekly real estate section in many regional and national newspapers. Many list the going rates for lenders in the area.

Term   Like interest rates, every extra year of your loan's life adds thousands to what you'll eventually pay. If you can afford the monthly payments, consider a fifteen- or twenty-year mortgage instead of the more common thirty-year term.

Prepayment   Make sure you're allowed to prepay your mortgage. Most lenders permit this, and because few people stay in the same home for the full life of the loan, you'll want to be sure you have this option.

Refinancing   All loans can be refinanced except those that forbid prepayment. Some loans have refinancing built in, with no requirement that you pay closing costs again. For instance, some variable-rate mortgages allow you to convert to a fixed-rate mortgage for a small fee at designated times. Find out about these options. They're especially helpful if you are forced to take a variable-rate loan because interest rates are high and you don't want to lock into a high fixed rate.

TRADITIONAL MORTGAGES

A conventional loan is an indebtedness or mortgage made between a lending institution and a borrower, without participation by a third party such as the VA or FHA (see Chapter 10).

Most conventional loans are paid off in equal monthly payments spread over fifteen, twenty, twenty-five or thirty years. The interest rate stays the same for the life of the loan, and the amount you pay each month also remains constant. When interest rates rise, a low fixed-rate mortgage is better for the borrower, but the lender finds it costly because the money loaned to you at a low rate could be earning higher interest. When interest rates go down, the borrower is better off with a flexible rate that takes advantage of the decline. The trouble is that no one can accurately predict future interest rate shifts. Borrowing money is always a gamble.

The advantage of conventional mortgages is that they usually involve relatively little red tape and can be processed quickly. A loan can be approved in as little as two to four days. (Look for lenders who advertise "speedy approval" if you're under a tight schedule.)

Until recently, the traditional fixed-rate mortgage was routine in home purchases, and they still make up a significant portion of all mortgages. The difficulty is that their rates are generally higher than the low initial rates of variable loans. But the certainty of knowing that the rate will never change is very attractive for many people. Rates do vary, however, so careful comparison shopping among lenders, their rates and other charges is advisable.

Private Mortgage Insurance (PMI)

One way to finance your loan with a low down payment is to purchase private mortgage insurance from your lender. Most lenders require such insurance to protect them against the risk of loans with less than a 20% down payment. Companies that offer PMI insure loans only at the market interest rate (see Chapter 10 for FHA and VA loan programs).

PMIs are simple. You pay the insurance company an annual premium to cover the lender's security requirement. The obligation normally runs out after seven years. If you're contemplating shopping for a government-backed loan, compare the cost of using PMI instead to obtain a loan with a low down payment.

GRADUATED-PAYMENT MORTGAGES

Some loans have a fixed rate of interest but obligate you to gradually increasing monthly payments. The early payments on the loan are lower even than the amount of interest that is due. Later payments are based on an increasing loan balance and are therefore larger. In effect, the longer you pay, the more you owe—for a while. Normally, payments rise for five to ten years, by which time they exceed the interest due on the loan, then level off as you begin paying off the loan itself.

Because payments are lower in the early years, graduated-payment mortgages may make sense to young buyers whose incomes may be relatively low now but who expect their earnings to increase steadily in the future. Remember the cost of this arrangement, however: the amount you don't pay in the early years serves to increase your total indebtedness. If you sell after only a few years, you could end up owing more than you borrowed in the first place. This is called *negative amortization.*

Tax Implications   Negative amortization makes graduated mortgages undesirable for those who plan to sell their homes within a few years. It also means your equity takes longer to build because you are paying only interest at first (and not even all of that). On the plus side, you'll get a large tax deduction on the interest you're paying. For most people, however, that isn't quite the bonus it may seem. For those with low incomes now, this interest deduction is not the benefit it would be to people in a higher income bracket. It will be a great disadvantage later, when they are earning more and could benefit from the deduction. When that time comes, they will be paying mostly the principal and only a declining amount of interest, the only payments that are tax deductible.

ADJUSTABLE-RATE MORTGAGES (ARMs)

The *adjustable-rate mortgage* (ARM) or *variable-rate mortgage* is a long-term mortgage with no fixed interest rate. At predesignated times, the lender adjusts the interest according to general market conditions, usually using a specific *index.* Some of the most commonly used are the U.S. Treasury Bill rate, the rate set by the Office of Thrift Supervision—the agency that regulates S&Ls—and the national average of mortgage interest rates.

Different kinds of adjustable-rate loans are available, and your choices will vary from one lender to another, so shop carefully. Also, when you shop for an adjustable-rate loan, it's best to describe the type you're looking for instead of trying to name it.

Always remember that lenders offer adjustable-rate loans to protect themselves—not you. They want to be able to increase the interest rate if and when general interest rates go up. They offer a number of features to entice you into paying these changing rates, so be careful to weigh all the advantages and risks when you compare one ARM with another or with a fixed-rate mortgage. The two most important things to find out are: what protection you will have against unpredictably high payments, and how the adjustments are handled.

A change in the interest rate, whether upward or downward, is generally reflected in the monthly payments you have to make. There may or may not be limits (*caps*) on how much the interest rate or the payments can be changed at any one time. Look for them and try to get them included in your mortgage.

Alternatively, the repayment schedule can be tailored to your needs. In other words, you can agree to make constant payments and let the balance of what you owe be adjusted up or down as rates change. If the rate is adjusted down over the long term, you'll repay the loan in less time. If it is adjusted upward, repayment will take longer.

One advantage of the ARM is that you usually can negotiate a below-market interest rate for a short period of time. For example, some lenders may offer loans for as low as 7% interest for the first year at a time when fixed rates are 10%. At the end of the introductory period, the loan's rate is adjusted to the current market rate, using one or a combination of the indices.

Because the initial rate may be low, an ARM is particularly attractive to the young, first-time home buyer who can't qualify for a fixed-rate mortgage. However, before committing yourself to an ARM, ask for some essential information:

Is There a Cap?   Does the adjustable-rate mortgage limit the rate of interest you'll have to pay? Does it limit the total potential monthly payment you'll have to pay? If interest rates climb again, you don't want to be caught having to make monthly payments higher than you bargained for.

What Kind of Cap? Lenders offer different kinds of caps. One is a *periodic* cap that limits how much the interest rate may change at any one time. For instance, it can require that even if the index increases 2% in one year, your rate can go up by only 1% in that year. Alternatively, an *aggregate* cap limits how much the rate can increase over the entire life of the loan. For example, even if the index goes up 10% in five years, your cap can limit your rate increase to 5% under an aggregate cap. Also watch for downward caps, which protect the lender's profits in times of declining rates. These work against you in that you will not get the entire benefit of falling rates.

You can also get a cap on payments, limiting the additional amount—to say, $500—that you'll have to pay in any given year, regardless what happens to interest rates. A cautionary note: even though your actual monthly payment increases only a little, if the interest rate rises significantly, the amount of your payment that is set against the interest rather than the principal increases and your equity payment shrinks. What could occur under a payment cap plan in a rising-interest economy is the same negative amortization danger that can result from a graduated-payment mortgage, discussed earlier: your monthly payment may be used entirely to pay interest. If it is not enough to cover the interest due, your indebtedness grows with each payment period.

Are There Prepayment Penalties? Some lenders charge a penalty to make up for some of the interest they lose when a borrower pays more than is required in a monthly payment. Most ARMs don't carry these prepayment penalties, but check to be sure.

You can get comprehensive information about ARMs from

lenders. Ask for a free copy of the booklet *Consumer Guide to Adjustable Rate Mortgages* published by the Federal National Mortgage Association (Fannie Mae).

Rollover Mortgages   A rollover mortgage is another version of flexible or adjustable-rate mortgages. With the rollover, the interest rate remains constant for a specified number of years, with the understanding that it will then be renegotiated. Make sure you understand early what the renegotiation will be based upon and when it will occur. Sometimes it will be renegotiated using some economic indicator, such as the treasury bill or prime rate; other times no indicator is used.

The rollover can be renegotiated to a lower rate, but in virtually every case the lender is in the driver's seat. This is because your only recourse as a borrower is to pay this loan off by getting a new one. If you go to a new lender to pay off the first, you may be almost forced to agree to the lender's terms. Before choosing a rollover, think about other options, especially variable-rate mortgages, which offer all the same advantages and few of the drawbacks.

BALLOON MORTGAGES

Some people say a good rule of thumb for when to agree to so-called *balloon mortgages* (or balloon formats of other mortgages) is "never, never, never under any circumstances." This is a little extreme, but it does reveal an important truth about this form of loan. It is extremely risky.

Under a balloon mortgage, your payments remain constant for a specified number of years, then end in a single, final "balloon" payment of the entire outstanding debt. In most cases, the balloon payment comes quickly, perhaps in three to five years. For those without a great amount of cash on hand, this final payment can be disastrous. People who may benefit from a balloon mortgage are probably using the house to shelter income and plan to sell it before the mortgage is paid.

Because it comes so soon after the loan is made, the final balloon payment can often amount to 70% to 80% of the original loan. Most people don't have that sort of money on hand. In response to this, some lenders offer automatic refinancing at the end of the balloon mortgage, but beware: you aren't guaranteed an interest rate and may end up having to choose between making a $50,000 cash payment and refinancing the loan at sky-high interest rates.

THE EVER-CHANGING MARKET

Recent years have brought many and fast-paced changes to home buying in America, particularly in the ways the purchases are financed: who loans the money, how much the loans cost, how they are repaid.

Interest on the loan you make to buy your home often costs more than the home itself. The affordable loan can still be found, but it is likely to be quite different from what used to be the conventionally financed arrangement.

In the past, once you found the home you wanted and could afford, financing it was routine. Today locating a suitable loan and getting approval for it can be arduous. Lenders have responded to the changing market by adjusting their business practices to protect themselves. As a result, even when you get a loan, it is unlikely to resemble the fixed-interest, fixed-payment loan package of yesterday.

After skyrocketing to more than 20% in the 1970s, interest rates returned to a relatively stable level, but there is no telling what tomorrow will bring. Inflation has also been less than the double-digit rates of the 1970s, but here too even the experts can't predict what will happen in the years ahead. One thing you can be sure of, however: lenders will respond to whatever market conditions exist by structuring loans in terms they find most favorable to themselves.

Be diligent in your search for the right plan and shop for your mortgage as carefully as you shop for the home itself. Many plans that seem affordable at first glance may be unrealistic.

Because finding the money to buy a home is often harder than finding a home to buy, you should be working on both at the same time. Neither effort should be made independently of the other. The two are dealt with in separate chapters, but that does not mean they are unrelated. From the time you decide to buy a home until you close the deal, you should continue to think about both.

CHAPTER 10

MONEYLENDERS

M ost home buyers turn to conventional lending institutions like banks and savings and loan associations, but you should be aware that other sources of obtaining financing are also available. These include the federal government and the seller.

Different lenders and different loan formats make different demands on borrowers. Conventional lenders who make fixed-rate loans require down payments that are higher than other loan formats require. Government-assisted loans, such as FHA and VA, have little or no down payment requirements. Community savings and loan associations (S&Ls) often require a *note of personal liability* in addition to posting your home as collateral. This means that if you fail to make your payments and the S&L sells your home to get its money back, you've agreed to make your other assets available to make up any loss that the sale of your home doesn't cover. The S&L also can transfer your note to a collection agency (or to anyone else, for that matter), which then takes over collecting from you.

Some lenders require that your loan be *nonassumable.* An assumable loan is one that can be transferred to a buyer when a house is sold. Its major benefit is that if it carries a low interest rate, that rate can be passed along to the new borrower even if prevailing interest rates at that time are higher. If you can arrange a loan with a low interest rate, having the ability to transfer your loan will make you an attractive seller later on.

Secondary Mortgage Market Many people have heard the nicknames Fannie Mae, Freddie Mac and Ginnie Mae. These are large lenders, some private, some government-operated, that buy loans from local and even regional lenders and sell them to investors on the secondary market. Without the ability to transfer loans to larger institutions, smaller lenders would soon run out of money to loan to other customers.

All this means for you, the borrower, is that your lender will expect your loan application to meet the requirements set by the "secondary" market. As noted earlier, for loans to be purchased by these secondary lenders, they must conform to industry rules on how much of your income you can devote to the mortgage and how much debt you can have (see Chapter 4).

Secondary market lenders vary, and if your lender tells you your situation won't be acceptable to its secondary lender, a different institution with a different secondary lender may have less restrictive rules. As always, shop around.

CONVENTIONAL LENDERS

Savings and Loan Associations The single largest source of private residential financing in the country is savings and loan associations. S&Ls offer several advantages. They are usually rooted in the community, they are generally relatively small operations that emphasize personal contact, and they can make a more knowledgeable appraisal of the property and neighborhood than can other lenders. S&L mortgages tend to have longer terms than others. They almost always require a note of personal liability, but they tend to go less "by the book" in their judgment of you as a credit risk then other lenders do.

They also have disadvantages, however. Their loans often cost more in fees and points, carry prepayment penalty charges and usually can't be transferred from you to a future buyer of your home at the same or similar interest rate—that is, they are nonassumable.

For those buying their first family home, S&Ls present an attractive option because they are interested in building goodwill and long-term customers in the community. This doesn't mean they'll accept wild credit risks, but it does give the first-time buyer a fighting chance to establish creditworthiness.

In 1989 the savings and loan industry underwent major challenges and changes. In response to frequent S&L failures usually caused by mismanagement and fraud, the U.S. Congress changed the way the institutions are regulated and managed. Formerly S&Ls were regulated by the Federal Home Loan Bank Board and insured by the Federal Savings and Loan Insurance Corporation. The 1989 law eliminated both these agencies and turned S&L regulation over to the Office of Thrift Supervision in the Department of the Treasury. Insurance was assumed by the Federal Deposit Insurance Corporation, which insures banks. Also, new regulations were enacted to restrict lending practices and the level of assets a lender needs to make loans.

Commercial Banks   The lending area of most commercial banks, even those that are locally based, extends farther than that of the typical S&L. The cost of making the loan may be lower than at an S&L, and because banks want your other banking business, they may be more lenient about such things as prepayment penalties.

The disadvantages are that commercial banks will probably charge slightly higher interest, they are unlikely to loan you as much money as an S&L and they favor shorter-term loans.

Credit Unions   These institutions are a good source of financing if you are a member and have little credit history outside of the credit union. Credit unions favor government-assisted loans and longer terms. Not all credit unions make mortgages, however, and those that do often don't have sufficient funds for financing large amounts of real estate.

Mortgage Companies   These companies "place" mortgages. They sometimes advertise low rates, speedy approval and flexible terms: fifteen-year loans, for example, or loans that can be paid in twenty-four annual payments. Often mortgage companies immediately sell your loan to a large bank or other investor on the secondary market. So if you like dealing with a local bank officer, you'd do better to look for lenders that keep their loans in the community.

There are also mortgage servicing companies that handle all the paperwork involved after the home is bought. These companies are often hired whether or not a loan is sold. They will provide the coupon books, send the statements of your taxable interest and even pay your taxes and mortgage insurance premiums.

MORTGAGE BROKERS AND BANKERS

Mortgage brokers match people with money, any money. They are not affiliated with any particular institution but may specialize in certain kinds of investments. Mortgage bankers, on the other hand work for "funds," large pools of money-lenders with large cash reserves.

Both know the market and can plug you in. Mortgage brokers and bankers can be especially helpful for borrowers on the edge of qualifying for conforming loans, those who have credit problems and those in a hurry.

Profits from these transactions come from commissions or, in some cases, from collecting payments and otherwise servicing loans. For this, they get a fraction of 1% of the outstanding balance owed.

Following are some of the sources of money that can only be accessed through mortgage brokers and bankers. Although you are more likely to use one of the sources we've already covered, it may be useful to consider mortgage bankers and brokers if it is hard to get a more customary mortgage.

Insurance Companies If the property you are buying is considered a "good investment" but is priced beyond what most lenders are willing to lend for it, you might be able to get financing from an insurance company. Insurance companies prefer to invest in large commercial development mortgages, often through mortgage brokers, so you'll have to sell them on the soundness of investment in your purchase. Your personal charm, local residence and other factors that might play a part in dealing with local banks and S&Ls will count for nothing in dealing with insurance companies. The only thing that counts is the wisdom of the investment. If you succeed in selling that, however, you may be able to save significantly on points, fees and interest.

Real Estate Investment Trusts (REITs) These special mortgage trust companies lend money on unusual deals and tend to be more flexible with loan features and gimmicks. They are a particularly good source of home construction financing and short-term loans. As with insurance companies, however, personal contact will have little influence.

Pension Funds and Endowments These groups, which have substantial capital to invest, usually buy mortgage "packages" from a mortgage broker. If you learn of one that offers terms that appeal to you—for instance, through a pension plan you belong to—by all means inquire.

PRIVATE MONEY

The unlikeliest source of all for financing a home is a private loan from a friend or family member. Not many individuals have the money it takes to finance a home purchase. Even when a person does have such money available, far more secure and profitable investments are available.

Nevertheless, a private loan can be a last resort. If you can't obtain financing elsewhere, ask a mortgage broker or real estate broker about private financing possibilities. Recognize, however, that such private money is much more likely as a source for your down payment or for the additional money you may need to make up the difference between the sales price and what an institutional lender is willing to loan you.

Many people borrow or are given money by family members for the down payment, then look to traditional sources of financing for the remainder. If you are given the money, you will be asked to submit a "gift letter" that certifies you will not have to pay the money back. If you are loaned the money, the lender will want to know this and will calculate it into your monthly debts when deciding whether you qualify for a loan.

COSIGNERS

First time home buyers or those with little credit history may be asked to have a family member, friend or employer cosign the mortgage. This means that if you fail to make your mortgage payments, your cosigner may be asked to pay. Such an arrangement should be used only as a last resort.

Typically, newly married couples buying their first home

are often asked to have a parent cosign a note and offer their own property as additional security. Don't be pressured into this sort of financial bondage unless you have no other way of getting a loan and your cosigners understand fully that they can be called upon to make good on the loan if you fail to make your payments.

GOVERNMENT-BACKED LOANS

Government-backed loans, usually supported by the Federal Housing Administration (FHA) or the Veterans Administration (VA), are in a special class called *assisted mortgages.* Unlike private lending institutions, government agencies have no claim on the future increased value of the property and provide help as a matter of public policy to encourage citizens to become homeowners.

The loans are not made by the government agencies themselves. Rather, the agencies give lenders assurances that they will be paid if you are unable to meet your payments. This is done by requiring you to buy insurance. If you default, the lender is covered for at least some of the loss.

For many people, homeownership is an unreachable dream without VA or FHA help. They simply cannot afford the down payment required for commercial loans. Information about how to apply is available at lending institutions and from the government agency offices themselves.

FHA Loans

The main attraction of an FHA loan is the low down payment and reduced initial costs of making the loan. Major disadvantages are bureaucratic delays and paperwork that make many lenders reluctant to deal with them.

The FHA has a wide variety of loan programs. For full information, check with local FHA-approved savings and

loan associations, commercial banks, mortgage bankers and mortgage brokers. These are the distinguishing features:
- Loans are fully assumable at their original interest rates and terms.
- The down payment is 5% or less, compared with a 10% to 20% requirement for most conventional loans.
- The FHA limits the loan amount it will back. The limit is based on the cost of housing in your area. The largest FHA loan amount is $124,875 in the highest-cost-of-living areas. Your lender will know the limit for your area.
- An FHA-approved appraisal of the value of the home is required. If the appraisal shows the property is worth less than the loan amount requested, you are not allowed to use a second mortgage to make up the difference.
- FHA loans may be prepaid without a penalty charge.

Until 1983 the government fixed interest rates for FHA loans. Since then it has allowed the rate to fluctuate with market conditions. As a result, the programs are now more attractive to lenders who, in the past, had been forced to charge the seller the lost interest percentage points in order to make a profit.

Lenders were forbidden to charge these points to the borrower. This often meant that sellers paid them instead and simply added the cost to the sale price of the house. The law now allows lenders to charge points directly to borrowers instead. Unfortunately from the buyer's point of view, FHA loans are usually accompanied by such a high number of points (four or five is not uncommon) that the up-front charges can offset the other advantages of FHA loans. An insurance premium payment ranging from 1% to 4% of the loan also is required up front.

VA Loans
Loans backed by the Veterans Administration (VA), also known as GI loans, are available to all current members of

the armed services and veterans who have served on active duty. Others can only get VA loans if they have a qualified veteran cosign.

The VA requires no down payment, but some lenders refuse to make any loan, government-guaranteed or not, without one. Also, some home buyers themselves choose to make a down payment to lower their monthly payments.

VA loans are available for just about any loan that is within the conforming loan level. They are like FHA loans in two important respects: they can be assumed by future buyers of the property at their original rates and terms, and they can be prepaid without penalty.

VA loans require a fee (approximately 1% of the loan) to be paid to the lender. The rates fluctuate with the market and, like the FHA loan program, points can be paid by the borrower.

Borrowers can apply for FHA and VA loans through regular lenders, who will have the forms you need and will know the loan limit, the going interest rate, the cost of necessary insurance, points and the length of time it will take for the application to be processed.

SELLER FINANCING

Home buying can also be financed by home sellers. In fact, second mortgages and other forms of seller financing accounted for more than half of all mortgages in 1980, when high inflation and high interest rates were making it difficult to find assumable fixed-rate loans. Lenders insisted on writing "due on sale" clauses into mortgage contracts to prevent subsequent buyers from assuming the mortgages at the old—and lower—interest rates. The availability of adjustable-rate mortgages has made such seller-financing arrangements less desirable, but they are still worth exploring.

If you are thinking about asking for seller financing, check with the seller's broker. In some markets, where interest rates are high and people aren't buying homes, the broker may even suggest this as a way of making a sale. You may find yourself with a seller willing to set up any of a variety of financing arrangements—assumption of the earlier loan, a wraparound or a second mortgage. If you decide or are asked to go this route, be sure to read some of the mortgage books listed in the bibliography, Appendix IV.

Assuming the Old Mortgage

If the property you're buying is already mortgaged, the seller is probably planning to pay off the mortgage as soon as you pay the purchase price. An alternative is to keep that mortgage alive by assuming the obligation to make the payments on it yourself. The major advantage is that you will maintain the interest rate that was set when the mortgage was first created—presuming it was lower than what you can get now.

Lenders who handle FHA and VA loans usually allow you to assume the seller's mortgage at the original interest rate. Those who offer adjustable-rate mortgages will do the same, but you should recognize that the interest will change periodically with market conditions anyway. Most conventional loans, however, have "due on sale" clauses that make the balance of the old mortgage due when the house is resold. This prevents direct assumption, but it doesn't prevent you from bargaining with the lender. You can ask for new terms on the old mortgage that net you a better deal than you would find elsewhere on an entirely new mortgage. For one thing, the original lender is likely to be favorably inclined because the value of the property involved is already known.

If the lender is willing to transfer the old mortgage to you with its original low interest rate, it will probably involve an extra charge. Whether this represents a net saving to you compared to taking out a new loan depends on the size of the charge and on how many years you will be paying the mortgage at the lower interest rate. Make sure you do your arithmetic before agreeing.

Because an assumable mortgage is usually attractive to buyers, it's also attractive to sellers—which you will be one day if you decide to sell your home. When you get your mortgage, whether it's a new one or an assumed one, always try to reserve the right to permit others to assume your mortgage if and when you decide to move on.

Wraparound Mortgages

One of the most common ways a seller can serve as your lender is to continue making payments on the old mortgage and to "lend" you the purchase price at a higher interest rate. This is known as a wraparound mortgage.

A wraparound might be made by a commercial lender or the seller. The idea is to take advantage of a low interest rate on an existing mortgage to reduce the amount of "new money" needed to complete the transaction.

For example, suppose the house you want to buy is priced at $100,000. The seller holds an 8% mortgage and still owes $50,000 on it. You give the seller $20,000 as a down payment and the seller keeps the existing mortgage in place and "lends" you the $80,000 you need at 10% interest, two percentage points below the market rate of 12%. The advantage to the seller is that you will make regular payments as if you had borrowed $80,000. Out of that, the seller makes the old mortgage payment at the original 8% rate and pockets the difference between what you pay and what is owed on the original mortgage.

Alternatively, a commercial lender could "buy" the original mortgage by giving the seller the $80,000 outright, then do the same thing—collect 10% from you and pay the original lender 8%.

The advantage of a wraparound mortgage to the buyer is that both the interest rate and the monthly payments may be less than they would be with a new mortgage. A potential disadvantage is that you may have no assurance the original loan will be paid unless those payments are handled by a commercial lender or some other third party such as an escrow agent. If the payments are supposed to be made by the seller and he or she fails to do so, you could find the original mortgage foreclosed and your ownership in jeopardy.

A further caution about wraparounds: the seller isn't subject to all the federal oversight, reporting regulations and recommended practices commercial lenders are. Recognize that you're gambling that you or your attorney can write a mortgage contract with the seller that will give you all the safeguards and remedies you expect from any lender, especially regarding late payments and foreclosure.

Second Mortgages

Another way sellers can help finance your purchase is by holding a *second mortgage,* also called a *second trust,* on the property. In effect, the seller loans you the part of the purchase price you couldn't find financing for and holds a mortgage for it. That mortgage is subject to the foreclosure rights of the holder of the first mortgage. In other words, if you don't pay your mortgage bills, the lender who holds the first mortgage is the one who has the right to take the property from you. Second mortgages are particularly well suited to buyers who have only a small amount of cash available for a down payment but have an assured monthly income high enough to handle payments on both mortgages.

CONCLUSION

This discussion of lenders and loans has described the more common types. If none of them meets your needs, consult the bibliography (Appendix IV) for additional sources of such information.

CHAPTER 11

GETTING
YOUR LOAN

$\mathbf{Y}$ou are now ready to apply for a loan. The following list covers the information you'll need for the loan application:

- Your annual wages and those of others in your household
- A description of other private income, such as from stocks, bonds, partnerships or royalties
- A written explanation of any large cash gifts you receive regularly
- Identification number and balance of each savings and checking account
- Account number and current balance of each credit card
- Account number of each certificate of deposit (CD), money market fund and security account and the value of those accounts as of a recent date
- A list of all outstanding installment debts and the amount and number of payments due on each loan
- If you already have a mortgage, the name of the mortgage holder, account number, monthly payment, original loan size, current balance and number of payments still due
- If you are the beneficiary of any trust, estate, IRA or Keogh plan, the cash value involved
- A written description of any lawsuit you are involved in and outstanding legal judgments for or against you
- A statement of your net worth—list the present market value of major holdings, such as your current home less

marketing costs and outstanding mortgages, the resale value of your car, stocks and bonds, the cash surrender value of insurance policies, and all other assets, list also your major debts, such as mortgages, automobile loans and credit card balances, then subtract what you owe from what you own; this is your net worth (see the worksheet on page 35)

If you're prepared with this information when you apply for a loan, it will both speed the process and impress the lender with your seriousness.

Remember, the lender will also get a credit report on you to see how you have handled past debts. You should check the report yourself first (see page 37).

SHOPPING FOR A LENDER

First determine which lenders in your area make loans of the size and type you want. For example, if you want an FHA or VA loan, find out which S&Ls and banks are willing to make them. This can be done by telephone or by talking in person with a loan officer where you bank.

Many regional newspapers have a weekend real estate section that lists the going rates for mortgages at the area's largest lenders. Consult this and then get on the telephone for the exact figures.

If you've been a regular customer of a bank or S&L, check there first. If your banker is willing to give you the type of loan you need at a price you can afford, your search may be short, but it's always wise to check with at least a few other lenders to compare prices. If your banker doesn't offer what you want, try the other sources of conventional and government-insured loans in your community. Determine the best loan for your needs and visit the appropriate lending institutions described in Chapter 10.

If you're still unsuccessful, try the institution where your employer, best friend, credit union co-members or church members bank. They may be willing to put in a good word for you. With such a recommendation, a bank or S&L may be a little more accommodating.

Many good lender-borrower matches are thwarted because people are so happy to find someone willing to "give" them the money they need that they jump at the first offer and look no further. Remember, whether or not you think you have a solid financial footing or an excellent piece of property, there is no reason to accept anything other than the best possible loan agreement. In the long run the loan agreement you buy can be far more important—and expensive—than the house itself. You can find the best agreement only by shopping diligently for it.

Be patient, careful and businesslike. Differences in the term and interest rate you agree to can have a dramatic effect on the total price you'll have to pay to borrow the money. A no-penalty prepayment option or an assumption option can mean literally thousands of dollars to you later on. Never jump at a loan just because it's available. If it's there today, it will still be there tomorrow. If it isn't, be suspicious. You even have a good chance of duplicating or improving on the offer at another institution down the street, so prepare to shop around. This is one case in which you hold more cards than you might think. Lenders want to make safe loans, true, but without borrowers they would make no loans at all—and earn no profits.

Using Professionals

Finding a lender may seem overwhelming, and it definitely requires some self-education. If you feel you need help, an array of professionals is prepared to offer it to you. Some you'll have to pay. Others you won't, at least not directly. They'll help you sort through the forms you need, assemble the numbers and come up with a workable plan. Many people who may find it hard to get financing and first-time home buyers will find these services helpful. You may especially want to consider the following two because they offer free help to borrowers:

Mortgage Broker   Instead of doing an exhaustive do-it-yourself search of the financial marketplace for the best loan, you can ask a mortgage broker to help you, especially if you've tried on your own without any success. The lender pays the mortgage broker a flat fee or a percentage of the loan it "places." They are paid to know the answers to all the routine questions: Where is money available? Which lenders are making what kinds of loan? What is the range of interest rates available? Is a bargain rate available on the size, type and term you're looking for? Which lenders' property or credit analysis will tend to favor your particular circumstance?

An experienced broker not only keeps up with changes in the local market but maintains working relationships with loan officers and other lending professionals. If you have proceeded on your own and have had no luck, don't give up before consulting a broker.

Clearinghouses   Thanks to modern technology, a one-stop method of mortgage shopping is also now available to home buyers—computer mortgage clearinghouses. These are relatively new institutions, but they are growing in popularity. At present there are only a few nationwide companies, but others operate regionally or locally. They are able to offer many times the number of loans and many more variations than other lenders can.

The information required and the information produced by the computer system depend on the company, but in general the clearinghouses work much the same way computerized dating services do—matching lenders and borrowers. The participating lenders in the area list their mortgage formats with the computer clearinghouse, including the amount they'll loan, their terms and their requirements. Information about your income, debts and cash on hand is fed into the computer. Based on this information, the maximum fixed-rate and adjustable-rate loans you qualify for are calculated and converted into the maximum price and down payment the computer thinks you can handle. Some systems offer you several alternatives and show you what would be available if your income or cash on hand were a little higher.

After the figures are produced, the computer prints out those mortgages it knows about that meet the requirements. In most cases these services are just a starting point and you still have to apply and be approved for a loan. However, in other systems, you choose the loan you want and your information is sent to the lender for approval. Some companies' computers are even programmed to print out the specific application for the loan you choose. Meanwhile, once the computer has made its initial evaluation the lender makes a provisional commitment to loan you a specified amount at a specified rate, contingent on an appraisal of the property and a check of your credit.

A major benefit to the system is that the borrower doesn't pay to use it, the lending institutions do. Your expenses are only those you would pay otherwise—the closing costs. Some clearinghouses even offer personal loan advice, and some can tell you the potential future costs of loans under different economic conditions.

The disadvantage is that most of the data banks do not include community savings and loan association mortgages. You will have to shop for those on your own. Also, any personal contacts that can be helpful in terms of moving a loan application along later down the road will not be useful here.

To use one of these services, ask the broker showing you around or your own broker if you have one. If you want just to call for general information, any real estate broker, mortgage banker or broker or lending institution can tell you which clearinghouses are available in your area. Some are accessible only to members of the profession or, in the case of the clearinghouse run by the National Association of Realtors, accessible only to its members.

THE LOAN APPLICATION

Sooner or later you'll have to take that step through the door of a lending institution. Whether it's a bank, credit union, S&L or insurance company, once inside, you will be directed to a mortgage loan officer. It is that officer's job to receive all requests, to separate the serious, qualified shoppers from the browsers and the clearly unqualified, and to process the loan application. (In some instances, if you have chosen a mortgage company and not a bank, you may meet with an officer at his or her home, your home or the office of a local real estate broker.)

The two of you will work together to fill out your loan application. When it's completed, the loan officer will submit it and a personal recommendation to a review board at the institution. The officer's recommendation is often crucial, unless the lending institution has strict rules about formal criteria for making loans.

Lenders consider both you and the property you're buying in their attempt to evaluate the risk you're asking them to take. The amount they rely on and how they analyze the various factors may, however, be open to negotiation. Your loan officer may be willing to share insights into your strengths and weaknesses with the review board, based on past performance, so don't be reluctant to ask.

Be aware that loan officers are not obliged to tell you all the standards and methods of analysis they use to evaluate you and your property, but they will often give you "ballpark" figures, or a profile of their "average borrower." If you don't come up to this standard, ask how flexible the loan officer thinks the board is.

The negotiation between you and the loan officer is just that—a bargaining session. The key is to find out how your application is perceived, then to discover if the perception of you as a loan applicant varies from one lender to another. It probably will.

Shopping for the best loan, or even negotiating better terms, isn't difficult once you understand what the loan officer is looking for in a borrower. By anticipating demands, you can satisfy them in a way that appears most favorable to your position. At that point the loan officer should be willing to listen to your loan preferences.

Some of the things to ask a loan officer about:

Amount Financed   This is the total amount of your loan. Make sure it is going to cover the cost of your home minus the amount of your down payment.

Annual Percentage Rate   This is the rate of interest you will pay. If your rate is fluctuating, find that out as well as the indicator that is used.

Finance Charge   This is the total amount of money you will pay in interest. When you combine this amount with the amount financed, you get the "total of payments," the amount you will pay if you keep your mortgage for its full life. The amount financed, annual percentage rate, finance charge and total of payments are costs of loans lenders are required to disclose to you on the *truth in lending disclosure statement,* which will be given to you immediately after you apply for your loan (page 141).

Prepaid Charges and Deposit   These are all one-time charges made by the lender before or at settlement. These items, discussed in Chapter 12, often include application, commitment, and loan origination fees; discount points; fees for assumptions, periodic inspections, or FHA contractors;

prepaid interest or insurance payments; and fees for preparing papers, such as the schedule of your payments.

Payment Amounts and Dates Unless you have a variable-rate loan or one that involves unequal or balloon payments, you should receive a simple schedule of how much you have to pay, how often, for how long and on what dates. Each payment amount will include a combination of the principal and the interest. In addition, unless you choose otherwise, many lenders will want you to have your property taxes and insurance "escrowed," meaning that you pay an additional amount with each monthly payment that the lender uses to pay your property taxes and premiums.

Late and Prepayment Charges The first is charged if you are late on a monthly payment, the second if you pay off the loan before its life is up. Ask how they are computed and when they must be paid. For the late charge, see if there is a five-, ten- or fifteen-day grace period. Most mortgages have these.

Paying off thirty years' worth of a loan early may not seem likely now, but you could win a lottery or receive an inheritance and want to pay it off ahead of time. In fact, the vast majority of people pay off their mortgages early because few people stay in one home for thirty years. Prepayment penalties can mean a substantial cost to you, so shop around to get a mortgage that has none or one in which the prepayment penalty lasts only for the first few years of the mortgage.

Lien Type and Extent You will want a clear statement about the sort of lien that will be placed on your property. If you default, under what terms can you redeem (get back) your property? What will the charges be?

Cancellation and Acceleration Policy This is related to payment amounts and dates. All loans are *callable* (the entire unpaid balance becomes due immediately) under certain conditions. Under what conditions your lender has the right to call your loan is crucial. When you miss two payments? Three? If you are late three times?

Assumability Policy   Can you transfer your mortgage to another borrower when you sell your home?

Other Costs   These costs usually include fees for the title search and insurance; charges for preparation of deeds, settlement statements and other documents; payments into a special account to cover taxes, insurance and utilities; fees for notary and credit reports; and any other inspection or application fees.

Locking In   Often you will not have to accept a specific rate of interest and points when you fill out the application. You will be permitted to "float" your loan. This means that after you apply, you will be allowed to call the lender each day and get the latest rates the lender is offering. (They change daily.) When you're ready, you choose the rate, locking it in, and get a statement confirming the rate. The lender will have a requirement as to how long after you lock in you must close or lose that rate. Make sure you choose your rate within a comfortable amount of time from closing.

CHAPTER 12

THE TITLE

When you buy a home, you are buying the seller's *title*—the right to possess, use, control and dispose of the property. The written legal evidence that the ownership rights have been transferred to you is a properly executed and recorded *deed.*

The Deed   The *deed* is a written document that, if properly drawn up and delivered, transfers title to real property from one owner to another. Different types of deeds convey different types of rights. Try to get the seller to agree in the purchase contract to give you a "warranty deed" and "good and marketable title." This means your title is "clear" and can be safely transferred to another. Getting a deed with this language, along with your title insurance and a survey, will protect your title against another's claim.

Sellers sometimes offer a *quitclaim deed,* also called a *contract of deed.* Be wary. Such a deed offers little protection to the holder. All you get with a quitclaim deed is the interest in the property that the seller owns, which may be no interest at all. Because the quitclaim contains no title warranties, you have no protection from title defects, such as improperly drawn boundaries or *mechanics' liens*—claims filed by contractors who were not paid for work they did on the property. Quitclaim deeds are often used for transfers between family members. Otherwise avoid them.

Decide ahead of time the form of ownership by which you want to take title. The consequences of tenancy in common, tenancy by the entirety and other forms of ownership were discussed in Chapter 1. State your preference in your contract of purchase so it can be transferred to the deed.

ASSURING TITLE

Getting and keeping title to your property is a three-step process: searching the title; buying title insurance; and buying extra coverage, called *endorsements*.

All your searching for the right home and the right financing will be in vain if the property you find doesn't have "good and marketable title." Unfortunately, this is the one area in which you probably can do little on your own to ensure that it does.

The real estate industry's system of deed registration, or the *chain of title,* can be searched to determine if your title is good, but this *title search* is such an archaic, complicated process, it cannot be done by the uninitiated, no matter how well prepared. The current system was created in fifteenth-century England under Henry VIII. It should be replaced with computerized record keeping similar to what is now used for automobile ownership records. Indeed, the sale and purchase of real property should be no more complicated than the sale and purchase of a car. The day of such simplification remains far in the future, however.

Title Searches
Despite the shortcomings, you have a way of assuring you are getting a good title. This involves a search of the records. For this you have to pay a separate charge from the title insurance policy premium. The price of this search varies widely, and can cost anywhere from $300 to $800.

Before the title insurance is issued, a title report is prepared, based on a search of the public records. The report, called a *certificate of title,* describes the property and identifies the owner, title defects, liens and encumbrances of record, including any judgments against the land. The company normally insures the title only after examining it for defects. If problems are discovered, the company can still insure the title, but it will require that certain conditions be met or make the insurance subject to specified exceptions.

Your best bet is to have the title company that is issuing the insurance also do the search. In some cases, however, the company that issues the insurance may accept one of the two options described below, review them and then insure the title. This is especially helpful if the attorney you hire to do your closing includes a title search in the fee. Don't be surprised, however, if title companies insure only titles they themselves search. Whatever you do, do not rely solely on one of the searches below. Get insurance.

Abstract and Lawyer's Opinion   The title assurance you get can be in the form of an *abstract* supported by an attorney's formal opinion or letter. An abstract is an historical summary of everything that affects ownership of the property and is available from the title company currently insuring the title. It includes not only the chain of owners of the property but also all recorded easements, mortgages, wills, tax liens, judgments, pending lawsuits, marriages and anything else that affects the title. When you buy the property, you can hire and pay an attorney to examine the abstract and give you a formal written opinion as to the validity of the title—including who the owner of record is and the lawyer's judgment of whether anyone else has any right to or interest in the property. This official opinion is known as the certificate of title. It too is to be paid for *in addition to* the cost of the title insurance. Typically, it can cost as little as $200 but can be higher depending on the number of past transactions that have to be described. Before you incur this expense, make sure your title company will issue insurance based on such a certificate. Many will not.

Attorney's Record Search   You (or the title company) can hire an attorney for a flat fee (typically $150–$400) simply to search public records and issue a certificate of title. This can be risky because, unless you buy title insurance, the only thing that protects you is the lawyer's malpractice insurance: if something goes wrong with your title, you can sue the lawyer's insurance company for damages—small consolation to those who have lost their "dream house." Again, ask the title insurance companies you're looking into if they will accept another lawyer's search.

Title Insurance

As noted above, the title company will most likely search the records and issue an insurance policy. This doesn't mean no one can ever claim ownership of your home, nor does it mean if someone does, you'll be assured you'll get to keep the home. What it does mean is that if at any time while you own your home someone else has a claim on it that should have been revealed in the title search, you will be reimbursed for your loss. The insurance pays if a conflict is later discovered that should have been found in the research into all of the previous owners of the property.

Your broker or agent, if you have one, will work closely with the title company. The company can issue either of two kinds of policies—a lender's policy, which covers only the lender until the mortgage is paid off, or an owner's policy, which covers you as long as you own your home.

Even though title insurance companies are regulated, the insurance rates vary enough to make it worthwhile to shop around. A one-time premium payment has to be made at the closing. The costs will vary depending on the value of the home you're buying. A good rule of thumb is $4 or $5 for every $1,000 of the purchase price. Special endorsements, discussed below, cost extra.

When you ask about title insurance companies and the fees they charge, also ask exactly what is covered in each case. Some routinely include the cost of handling the closing, the title search, title report and insurance protection.

If you're getting a new mortgage, the lender will probably make you buy a lender's title insurance policy, both to protect the lender's claim (*lien*) on the property and to make the mortgage an attractive enough investment to sell to mortgage bankers in the secondary mortgage market. Be aware, however, that the lender's policy doesn't protect *you*. To protect yourself you must buy an owner's policy and pay extra for it, or buy in an area where sellers customarily provide title insurance for buyers. If you do have to get both your own and your lender's title insurance, it's usually cheaper to buy them from one company and at the same time.

In general, title insurance policies have two parts. Schedule A includes a description of the property, your name, the seller's name and the amount of the insurance. Schedule B is more important. It lists what is excepted from the coverage. It can specify that the following conditions are not covered: unrecorded leases, mechanics' liens, unrecorded easements, utility company easements and rights-of-way and most other encumbrances and liens.

Schedule B and other policy exceptions may include:
- *Zoning.* They do not protect against the effects of zoning changes.
- *Eminent domain.* They do not accept responsibility if the government takes your property through its power to seize it for a public purpose, provided you are paid a reasonable price.
- *Claims.* They do not protect against defects, liens, encumbrances and other claims that are discovered after buying the property.

- *Errors.* The insurer may omit coverage for errors in the title search. This is especially likely when an outside lawyer does the search.
- *Inflation.* The insurer covers you only up to the amount of the property's existing value at the time of purchase. You will have to ask for and pay for additional coverage for increases in the property's value—a worthwhile expense.

If any of these exceptions holds, your title will be unmarketable and you could lose your home. The way to get around this is to purchase endorsements from your title company that negate these exceptions to coverage. It is usual to do this.

Endorsements

Almost all title insurance policies follow a standard format. Take time to read yours. If possible, have someone knowledgeable go over the details with you before closing. Pay close attention to what your policy covers and what it doesn't.

If you want coverage for something that is excepted in Schedule B, you can get an *endorsement* or *affirmative insurance* to delete that exception, but you will have to pay extra for this and meet requirements set by the insurer. The requirements will depend on which of the exceptions is being deleted. You may have to provide affidavits about possession, surveys, easements, liens or special assessments. Getting around exceptions by using endorsements is usually a matter for negotiation, so if you want them, ask for them in your preliminary discussions with the insurer.

You should get endorsements that remove exceptions for faulty boundaries and property lines, zoning and restrictive covenant changes, eminent domain, errors in the title search, mechanics' and other liens and inflation, plus a catchall Schedule B endorsement.

OTHER TITLE COMPANY SERVICES

When you hire a title company, you often get not only insurance but a number of other services. Don't be surprised to hear "The title company usually takes care of that." Title companies are hired to prepare and register the deed and do all of the paperwork necessary to effect the transfer, including filing and paying taxes and submitting materials to the lender. They also insure the title after closing. There may be additional services. Be sure to ask and shop around for the best deal.

Reissue Policy   One way to save money and still receive full protection is to ask where the seller has title insurance and whether you can assume it at a reissue rate. In many cases a reissue can be obtained at a lower rate, sometimes even from a company other than the original insurer.

CHAPTER 13

CLOSING
THE DEAL

When you have struck a deal with a seller and found your financing, it's time to pay for the property and receive the deed. There is no standard name for this step. Depending on where you live, it may be called the *closing, title closing, settlement,* or *escrow.*

SETTLEMENTS AND ESCROW

Often the closing takes place at a meeting of all those involved. When that happens, the process is commonly called a *settlement.* If no meeting occurs, it's more often known as *escrow* and is handled by an *escrow agent.* In such cases, the buyer and seller usually sign an agreement to deposit certain funds and documents with an escrow company, which acts as agent for both sides. When all the papers and funds are in, the escrow is *closed* and the agent records the documents and makes the appropriate payments.

Settlement, however, involves much more than the formal acts of *passing the papers.* All the details, loose ends and additional services required to conclude the deal must be tended to. This is when the full cost of buying a home becomes clear—not just the purchase price or the cost of the loan to buy it, but the actual costs of the process of buying as well. Be warned: these closing costs can add up to 8% of

the purchase price of the home. As the buyer, you can expect to pay 3% to 6% of this sum.

BEFORE THE CLOSING

Between the day you sign the contract and the day you
take title, you need to attend to other details besides your
mortgage, title search and title insurance arrangements.

If you feel the seller may not honor part of the contract
after the closing, don't count on litigation as a practical solu-
tion to your problem. Insist instead that the seller leave a
deposit in a special account for several months to protect
the terms of the contract. Should the seller fail to live up to
the contract, the deposit will be turned over to you.

For example, if the seller has agreed to cart away debris
from the basement but has been unable to schedule the
hauling service, you should ask that an amount equal to the
cost of doing so be put away to ensure it happens. The other
alternative is to ask that your purchase price be reduced by
the amount you will have to spend, then hire the hauling
service yourself.

If a survey was not done by your lender, have the property
surveyed if you have any doubt about its boundaries. Check
with the clerk's office at your county courthouse to be sure
no outstanding liens or lawsuits are pending against the
seller that might result in the property being seized or attached. In many areas these tasks are handled by the title
insurance company in the course of doing the title search.
Ask your title searcher if they were included.

THE FINAL INSPECTION

This is commonly known as a "walk-through" and should
be done with a suspicious eye toward all of the verbal and

written promises made about the property, including all fixtures and appliances. This also may be the first time you get to see the home with little or no furniture in it because the seller may have started moving or at least packing to move. Look around and make sure no surprises were hidden behind furniture. Check again for defects and last-minute removal of fixtures you expected to remain with the property. This is not the time for a professional inspection or checking the condition of specific things, such as appliances. That should have all been done during earlier inspection visits.

If you're buying a newly built home, get a certificate of completion of construction from the local government's building or health departments. Also make sure all utilities have been turned on. Finally, review, or have someone review for you, the plans and building specifications to make sure the construction is in full compliance.

CLOSING COSTS

The key to a successful settlement is to get estimates of your charges as early as possible. You should have received rough estimates when you first started shopping for a loan, but once your purchase offer is accepted, you should have more detailed estimates from both the sales agent and the lenders to whom you applied for a loan.

Your lender will have given you a "good faith estimate of closing costs" soon after you applied for the loan. You also have the right to receive, at least one day before closing, a settlement statement on a HUD-approved form that lists all the closing costs. These may change a little because of last-minute messenger charges or other miscellaneous fees, but it should be pretty accurate when you receive it. HUD's *Special Information Booklet* contains very detailed explanations about many of these potential closing costs.

The Special Information Booklet   To assist home buyers and to protect them, the U.S. Department of Housing and Urban Development has published the *Special Information Booklet.* It is a clear, straightforward message to consumers about the specific rights and remedies they have in their dealings with the professionals of the real estate industry. It also contains an excellent reproduction of a settlement statement, with each cost explained. Get it and use it as a reference when you receive your settlement statement. It will explain much of what you need to know about each charge.

Law requires that all lending institutions give a copy of the *Special Information Booklet* to anyone who applies for a home loan. Lenders may put their own cover on the booklet, but they may not alter its text. Also, the cover must by law include the words "settlement costs," for example: "HUD's Guide to Settlement Costs" or "Your Guide to Settlement Costs."

You need not wait until you apply for a loan to get a copy. The *Special Information Booklet* is included as part of a HUD publication entitled *Real Estate Settlement Procedures Act,* a sixty-four-page guide to buying a home. A copy can be purchased by calling or writing your regional office of HUD (see Appendix II) or by writing to the Consumer Information Center, P.O. Box 100, Pueblo, CO 81009.

Your settlement costs are influenced by, among other things, what county you live in, how you financed your purchase and what your lender required before making you the loan. Local custom influences whether the buyer or the seller pays any particular charge. This is why it is important that your purchase contract state explicitly who pays what. In some areas the buyer pays for title insurance because the buyer's lender requires the protection. In others the seller absorbs that charge as a selling cost. Sometimes the buyer pays the *recordation tax,* sometimes the seller does. The same is true of points.

The largest part of your settlement costs will be the lender's fees for your loan. These fees—the points—were discussed in Chapter 9. If the down payment and loan don't cover the entire cost of the property plus the buyer's share of expenses listed below, you must be prepared to make up the difference. Additional charges you may be asked to pay are included here. If you don't understand them or feel they are not applicable to your situation, discuss the matter thoroughly with the lender before proceeding.

Of the following potential closing costs, many go to the lender and some go to the seller, while others are paid to the title company, inspection company, and so forth. Some will apply to your purchase, others won't. Most fees paid to the lender are paid by the buyer, but again, this is negotiable and will turn on local custom. Some of these fees will be deductible from your income taxes. Consult with an accountant.

Charges Paid to the Lender

Points, Origination Fee, Commitment Fee   Prepaid interest. They increase the lender's initial intake to cover the administrative costs of making the loan.

Appraisal Fee   Payment for the lender's appraisal.

Credit Report Fee   Reimburses the lender for getting a copy of your credit history.

Inspection and Survey Fees   Reimburses the lender for these services.

Title Insurance   The premium that protects the lender. It may be paid directly to the title insurance company.

Interest   Interest for every day between closing and the date the first mortgage payment is due.

Attorneys' Fees   Payment to lender's lawyer to review all the papers.

Down Payment   Paid now, this sum goes to the seller.

Assumption Fee   If you're assuming the seller's loan or doing any kind of seller financing, the lender will have fees that must be paid.

Mortgage Insurance   If required, or if you chose to buy it, you usually are required to pay two or three months' premiums up front at the closing. The money goes into an escrow account the lender uses to pay the premium when it's due.

Property Taxes   Whether you escrow your taxes with the lender or not, you will be asked to deposit with the lender enough money to cover two or three months' property taxes.

Hazard Insurance   This is required by the lender to cover the cost of one year's insurance against loss from fire or natural disaster. After that, most people buy homeowner's insurance. Check what your hazard insurance covers so you don't duplicate the coverage during the first year you own the home.

Taxes

Transfer or Recordation Taxes   This state fee is paid, usually to the title company, whenever property is transferred. Local custom dictates who pays and the exact name will vary in each state.

Recording Fee   This fee for filing the deed is also paid to the title company for handling this task.

Other Fees

Inspection Fee   If you hired a professional inspector you have not already paid, the fee may be included here.

Survey Fee   If you had your own survey done, it may be included here.

Title Insurance and Search   The insurance premium will be paid here to the title company. If you hired a title company that included the search in its overall price, it may be a single charge for both the work and insurance. If you hired a separate lawyer to do the search or abstract, you may have to make two separate payments.

Assessments   These are charges you might owe the seller if you are moving in the middle of the month. For instance, it includes any part of the month's condo or co-op assessment or utility bills that the seller paid through the end of the month but that you will get use of. Prepaid taxes will be similarly apportioned.

Termite, Flood Inspections   Each state and county has its own regulations about what is required. Hazard insurance will cover some things, but the inspections here are additional. For example, in flood-prone areas an inspection will certainly be required. These charges may be the responsibility of the seller, buyer or the title company, depending on local custom.

Brokers' Commissions   The seller's broker and any buyer's broker fee must be paid.

Attorneys' Fees   If you or the seller hired an attorney to review documents, that may be paid for at this time, or you may be billed later.

Closing or Escrow Fee   If you and the seller split the costs of the paperwork through an escrow or closing agent, this fee will be divided between you.

Miscellaneous Fees   Document preparation, notary fees and messenger fees will all be separated out. Local custom dictates who pays, but don't be surprised if it all ends up in the buyer's column at closing. Still, who pays these fees is negotiable.

KNOW THE PLAYERS

If yours is going to be a traditional closing, expect a large gathering. In addition to yourself, those present may include the seller, the seller's lawyer, your lawyer, agents, the lender, the title insurance representative and the closing agent. Understand the role of each before the meeting so that during the meeting you can focus your attention on the procedures.

Settlement Agent   Someone will be on hand to orchestrate the give-and-take of money and papers. This normally is an employee of the title company. As noted earlier, title companies do a lot more than insure titles; among other things, they also perform closings. Expect to see a title company representative at the closing armed with all the papers. He or she may be sitting at the head of the table and running the show.

Title Insurance Representative   The sole purpose of this individual may be to present the title insurance policy to the owner, lender and buyer and ensure that all of the descriptions and figures are correct. Or this person could coordinate the closing and play the role of the closing agent. It depends on how he or she was hired.

Lawyers and Agents   The lawyer's role is to protect and advise the client, whether the seller, buyer or both, on the charges the client pays and the documents the client signs. If you have hired a buyer's agent, he or she should be able to represent you without an attorney. You can represent yourself, but if you choose to do so, prepare well. You'll be in a room full of professionals who know precisely what they're doing. Also, before deciding to go it alone, it's best to inquire about local custom: if self-representation in your area violates long-standing custom, you may want to reconsider.

AT THE CLOSING

In many parts of the country, the procedures at closing have become less of a personal exchange in recent years. Often buyer and seller don't even meet. The buyer simply receives the signed deed and a statement of closing costs by mail from the lender or title company. However, whatever the outward changes, the legal considerations and significance of the documents involved have not changed. What follows is a general description of the exchanges that take place at settlement, whether in person or by mail.

The lender, title company representative or broker hands over the mortgage papers for you or your agent or attorney to examine. If they are in order and contain no surprises, you sign them. Check all addresses and numbers closely.

You then get a check for the amount of the loan. If the mortgage is guaranteed by the VA or FHA, you also get VA or FHA loan forms to sign.

The title company produces the title insurance policies that protect the lender, and you if you purchased it, against defects in the title. These are checked against the description of the property in the deed and against the survey, if one was made.

If the home you are buying is new, the builder may be present and give you a certificate of occupancy, a document issued by the local government. It states that the house was built in accordance with local regulations and with the plans submitted for approval before construction. (Some cities or counties require certificates of occupancy for all homes, old and new.) The builder also hands you whatever written guarantees of materials and work were specified in the purchase contract. Examine these papers to be sure they accurately reflect what you expected.

The seller or the seller's lawyer hands over the deed for examination by you, the lender and the title company representative. It should already be in your name. The written description of the property in the deed should be carefully compared with what is in your purchase contract, with any surveys that were done by you or by the title company, and with descriptions in earlier deeds to the same property examined by the title company in its search. This is your last chance to make sure you're getting exactly the property you expect to own and under exactly the terms you negotiated. This is not the time for surprise revelations.

When you are satisfied the deed is properly drawn, the seller signs the deed and hands it to you. Endorse the lender's check over to the seller and give the seller your check for any balance you still owe on the purchase price. This sum is usually the down payment plus fees.

The escrow agent, title company representative or seller's lawyer and you or your lawyer will have calculated how much each side owes toward divided expenses, such as real estate taxes and fire insurance. The settlement papers will have two columns of figures, one for the seller, one for the buyer, listing all the closing costs with totals at the bottom. From these totals the final payments will be determined. One person, usually whoever is orchestrating the closing, will have a bank account for depositing and writing checks. At this time the checks are written, signed and handed to the appropriate party.

The seller or broker will already have your deposit, and you can use that to offset any money you owe. The seller's broker will make out the correct check, returning your deposit with interest. If you need additional money, you can probably pay from your regular checking account. Bring your checkbook, but check the day before with the escrow agent or the seller's broker to make sure a certified check is not required.

You or the representative of the title company must see to it that the deed and mortgage are recorded with the proper authority as soon as possible after the closing. After the closing you'll be sent a summary of the transaction, called the closing statement.

Closing Problems Among people's greatest nightmares is an argument arising over some unexpected closing cost that causes the deal to fall through. Your best insurance against this is to go over carefully the estimates of closing costs you receive the day before. Read them over on your own or with your representative. Call the seller, the seller's broker or the closing agent if you have questions. Try to leave nothing to be decided at the closing except who pays for the doughnuts and coffee.

That concludes the purchase: you now officially own your new home.

CHAPTER 14

CONSUMER RIGHTS IN LENDING

Consumer awareness and pressure have brought about a broad range of regulatory mechanisms to restrict corrupt, illegal and deceitful activity in the housing marketplace. These include the Real Estate Settlement Procedures Act (RESPA), the Truth-in-Lending Act, the Unfair Trade Practices Act, certain Office of Thrift Supervision regulations governing savings and loan associations and the Home Mortgage Disclosure Act.

RESPA

The Real Estate Settlement Procedures Act (RESPA) requires that almost all private-home purchases that involve financing must include a series of disclosures that protect you from paying high fees for poor service. Following are the major provisions:

Special Information Booklet When you apply for a loan, the lender must give you a copy of the *Special Information Booklet,* published by the U.S. Department of Housing and Urban Development (HUD). Read this booklet carefully, cover to cover, as soon as you get it. Better yet, get a head start by getting a copy from a HUD regional office or by writing to the Consumer Information Center, Box 100,

Pueblo, CO 81009. The booklet explains in detail all your rights with respect to lending and closing practices. It also provides work sheets, forms and detailed information about all possible closing costs.

"Good Faith" Estimate The lender is also required to give you a good faith estimate of the closing costs you'll have to pay at settlement. This should be based on the size of your mortgage and the specific services the lender's system requires you to pay for. The lender has to get this information to you within three days of receiving your loan application.

Referrals The lender is allowed to suggest, or even require, that you buy particular services from specific vendors, but in some cases, unless you are allowed to choose from at least two sources for any given service, the lender must formally disclose to you information about the recommended vendor. You must be told the full name, address and telephone number; the fee charged for particular services; and whether or not the lender has a business relationship with that provider. Unfortunately, the requirement applies only to title services, legal work and the use of a particular person to conduct the closing.

RESPA also outlaws kickbacks or unearned fees for referrals. One way lenders get around this protection, however, is for the recommended service provider to maintain large interest-free accounts at the bank or S&L that is referring clients. The "fee" earned by the bank is the interest it doesn't have to pay on the account. Always ask if a recommended provider maintains an interest-free account with the lending institution that is handling your financing. If you uncover an illegal arrangement between a lender and any service provider you're told you have to use, you can sue for three times the size of the fee you're charged. Report any violations you suspect to your HUD regional office (see Appendix II).

Advance Settlement Statement   The day before closing you have the right to see an advance copy of the Uniform Settlement Statement, the government form used to record the costs of all settlements under RESPA. This statement must be used regardless of who conducts the closing. It is designed to conform with the analysis of lender costs and practices in the *Special Information Booklet*. The advance disclosure and your day-before preview are intended to eliminate the surprises and dismay home buyers used to encounter at settlement. The statement is an estimate of all closing costs, and as described in Chapter 13, it sets out all the costs in two columns.

TRUTH IN LENDING

The U.S. government has enforced truth-in-lending laws since passage of the Consumer Credit Protection Act of 1968. When applied to RESPA transactions, the law requires those who make loans as a business to give borrowers crucial information in a standard format that allows them to compare offers. The lender is required to give you this statement free of charge.

HOME MORTGAGE DISCLOSURE ACT

The Federal Reserve Board is responsible for investigating *redlining* practices under the Home Mortgage Disclosure Act. Redlining is the discriminatory refusal to make loans in neighborhoods populated by minority groups. Its name derives from the practice many lenders once had of outlining in red on a map those neighborhoods they felt were too risky to do business in. If you have reason to believe that redlining has occurred, contact the nearest Federal Reserve Board office, listed in your telephone directory under "U.S. Government."

If you are dealing with a savings and loan, the Office of Thrift Supervision has ruled that under the Disclosure Act, you must be given full information on all charges related to required legal services valued at $100 or more, including who will perform the services and whether they will benefit you or only the lender.

In recent years, the Federal Trade Commission (FTC) has been investigating the residential real estate industry. Send any complaints you have to the FTC, listed in your telephone directory under "U.S. Government," if:

- You are not getting full disclosure of important information
- You are having to contend with what you consider unfair or deceptive forms or practices
- You suspect collusion among the various professionals with whom you have to deal
- You believe your rights have been violated in any way

FAIR HOUSING LAWS

Fair housing laws protect all citizens against residential housing discrimination of any sort. You are guaranteed the right to buy, rent, deal or negotiate and receive the same terms and conditions as anyone else. You must be told when housing is available for inspection, rental or purchase, and no lender or service provider may conduct any real estate negotiation that in any way violates your civil rights. The law prohibits all practices that discriminate among customers and potential customers because of race, color, creed, religion or national origin.

CONCLUSION

 A s with all large investments, the process of buying a home should not be entered into without careful preparation. Study this book carefully, use experts as it seems necessary. As you enter the housing market, review and bear in mind the following general considerations.

 Prepare carefully, and know the role of each professional you deal with. Careful preparation is necessary, especially in arranging your financing and in contract negotiations. The complexity of the transactions involved in a home purchase makes it inevitable that you will have to deal with professionals at just about every stage—real estate brokers, lawyers, bankers, closing agents, inspectors, appraisers, title insurers and others. To save money and make sure your investment is a sound and safe one, you must understand the role of each of these professionals, whether or not you choose to employ them. The more you prepare, the more confidently you will deal with them.

 Watch for trends in the mortgage market. This manual discusses the recent and continuing revolution in the mortgage market in some detail. The number of options for financing increases each year, and the popularity of any one option rises and falls with changes in the housing market and the greater economy.

 One thing is certain: adjustable-rate mortgages are here to stay, regardless of the state of the economy, because interest rates now change more rapidly than they once did. Lenders wish to protect themselves from the fluctuations, both with adjustable rates mixed adjustable/fixed-rate loans, and with stricter credit guidelines.

Nationwide building standards have been abolished. The Federal Housing Administration (FHA) has ended the setting of uniform standards for housing. It will now be up to states, counties and local communities to establish such standards. It is especially important, therefore, that you very carefully inspect or have an expert inspect the home you want to buy for structural failures and other problems.

REFORMING THE SYSTEM

Despite its complexity, most of the work involved in title searches and settlement is routinely performed by non-professionals. It rarely consists of more than verifying items on a checklist and completing standardized forms. Complications in property transfers rarely arise. Less than 5% of all property transfers develop complications, and those are usually easily resolved. However, studies have revealed that home buyers are often charged for closing work that was, in fact, done several years earlier for a previous buyer.

The complexity of the system is needless. It seldom benefits anyone but the professionals who sell their ability to untangle it. Transferring real property can and should be simple and inexpensive. The use of intermediaries would be less costly—and often unnecessary—if procedures for transferring and recording real estate were simplified. Most countries in the industrialized world long ago instituted a land registration system in which the transfer of real property is as simple and as inexpensive as the transfer of an automobile is in the United States.

Consumers do have one ray of hope, however. It is that computerization of the land title system, recently pioneered by Wisconsin and a few other states will spread to more states.

There is little reason why everyday legal transactions cannot and should not be handled without the help of professionals. This is as true in the real estate marketplace as in other arenas that involve the routine application of law. However, for this to occur, more education of the general public is essential. Laws and regulations must be drafted in plain language, and unnecessarily complex and cumbersome procedures must be simplified.

APPENDIXES

INSPECTION LIST

The U.S. Department of Housing and Urban Development (HUD) (see Appendix II) can direct you to recommended inspectors in your area or supply you with its own printed materials. Whether you decide to hire a professional inspector or not, you should make a personal inspection, making sure to check the following:

Outside

Foundation: Look for holes, cracking, unevenness.

Brickwork: Look for cracks, loose or missing mortar.

Siding: Look for loose, missing, lifting or warping pieces.

Paint: Look for peeling, chipping, blistering, and so on.

Entrance: Examine steps, handrails, posts, and porch flooring for loose or unsafe features.

Windows: Look for cracked or broken glass, holes in screens. Check caulking for cracks and dried or falling-out sections. Are window frames warped, peeling or cracking?

Storm windows: Are they complete? Are they secure? Is the caulking fresh and complete?

Roof: Look for worn or bald spots; ask how old the roof is and whether it is under warranty. Check for missing shingles, tiles or slate, cracked or dried tar. Look for dampness and signs of water damage inside, especially near worn spots.

Gutters: Check for missing sections, gaps, holes in joints, signs of leaks.

Chimney: Look for tilting, loose or missing bricks.

Fences, walls: Look for holes, loose or missing sections, rotted posts.

Garage: Check doors, roof, siding and windows as above.

Driveway: Look for potholes and cracked pavement.

Landscaping: Locate the property line. Are trees, shrubbery and lawn in good shape?

Drainage: Will rain or snow flow away from the house? Do muddy areas indicate possible problems with septic tanks, underground leaks of water, sewage? (Visit during a rain storm if possible.)

Inside

Structure: Jump up and down on the floors. Does the house feel solid? Check support posts and floor supports in basement for looseness, bending, dampness, rot, termites.

Floors: Check for levelness, bowing, movement when you walk.

Walls: Check for major cracks, loose or falling plaster, leaks, stains.

Stairs: Look for loose treads, handrails, posts.

Plumbing: Check pipes and sewer lines for leaks and rust. Flush all toilets. Turn faucets on and off to test water pressure. Look for clogged or sluggish drains, dripping faucets.

Heating: Is the house heated by warm air, hot water, electricity or steam? What type of fuel is used? How much does it cost to heat? Ask for last year's fuel bills. When was the system last serviced?

Hot water heater: Check for leaks and rust. What is the capacity or "recovery rate?" (This should be at least thirty gallons for a family of four.) How old is the water heater?

Electricity: Does the "service box" use fuses or circuit breakers? Does it look old or new? Look for exposed wires and signs of wear.

Cooling: Is there a cooling and air-conditioning system? What is its age and condition? Is it under warranty? How much did it cost to operate last year? Ask for last year's utility bills.

Storage: Does the home have enough closets? Are they in appropriate locations, including near front and rear entrances? Can you use other areas or rooms for storage?

Windows: Open and close each one. Do they operate easily? Check for broken sash cords, loose or warped frames, locks and latches.

Doors: Do they close properly? Are the locks sound?

Layout: Are the rooms conveniently located? What are the traffic patterns between bedrooms and bathrooms, kitchen and dining area, living room and bathrooms?

Kitchen: What appliances are included (stove, refrigerator, dishwasher, garbage disposal)? Check their age, workability. Is there enough cabinet and counter space? Enough electrical outlets? Leaks under the sink?

Bathrooms: Are there enough for your immediate and anticipated needs? Check for cracks in tiles and leaks. How long does it take to get hot water? Is there a window or fan for proper ventilation?

Living room: Is it large enough for your immediate and anticipated needs? Is there a fireplace? If so, does the damper work? Check for signs of discoloration of walls and fabrics from smoke. Has the chimney been cleaned recently?

Bedrooms: How many are there? Are they large enough for your present and anticipated needs? Does each have a window to the outside (a requirement in some states or countries)? Does each have a large enough closet?

Basement: Check for leaks, dampness, flooding. Is there enough lighting?

Attic: Look for signs of roof leaks. Check insulation. How much is there? Look for signs of nesting by birds, squirrels, other rodents.

HUD OFFICES

The Department of Housing and Urban Development (HUD) is the agency responsible for administering federal programs related to the nation's housing needs. The Fair Housing Office administers the program authorized by the Civil Rights Act of 1968 and is chiefly concerned with housing problems of lower-income and minority groups. The Office of Neighborhoods protects consumer interests in all housing and community development activities and enforces the laws regarding interstate land sales, mobile home safety standards and real estate settlement procedures. For information, publications, advice, referrals or complaints about local housing practices, contact the regional office nearest you.

Region I
(Connecticut, Maine, Massachusetts, New Hampshire, Rhode Island, Vermont)
Department of Housing and Urban Development
10 Causeway St., Room 375
Boston, MA 02222
(617) 565-5234

Region II
(New Jersey, New York, Puerto Rico, Virgin Islands)

Department of Housing and Urban Development
26 Federal Plaza
New York, NY 10287
(212) 264-8053

Region III
(Delaware, Maryland, Pennsylvania, Virginia, West Virginia)
Department of Housing and Urban Development
Liberty Square Bldg.
105 S. 7th St.

Philadelphia, PA 19106
(215) 597-2560

Region IV

(Alabama, Florida, Georgia, Kentucky, Mississippi, North Carolina, South Carolina, Tennessee)
Department of Housing and Urban Development
Richard B. Russell Federal Building
75 Spring St. SW
Atlanta, GA 30303
(404) 331-5136

Region V

(Illinois, Indiana, Michigan, Minnesota, Ohio, Wisconsin)
Department of Housing and Urban Development
526 W. Jackson Blvd.
Chicago, IL 60606
(312) 353-5680

Region VI

(Arkansas, Louisiana, New Mexico, Oklahoma, Texas)
Department of Housing and Urban Development
1600 Throckmorton
Fort Worth, TX 76113
(817) 885-5401

Region VII

(Iowa, Kansas, Missouri, Nebraska)
Department of Housing and Urban Development
Professional Building
1103 Grand Ave.

Kansas City, MO 64106
(816) 374-6432

Region VIII

(Colorado, Montana, North Dakota, South Dakota, Utah, Wyoming)
Department of Housing and Urban Development
Executive Tower Building
1405 Curtis St.
Denver, CO 80202
(303) 837-4513

Region IX

(Arizona, California, Guam, Hawaii, Nevada)
Department of Housing and Urban Development
450 Golden Gate Ave.
San Francisco, CA 94102
(415) 556-4752

Region X

(Alaska, Idaho, Oregon, Washington)
Department of Housing and Urban Development
Arcade Plaza Building
1321 Second Ave.
Seattle, WA 98101
(206) 442-5414

For General Information

Office of Public Affairs
U.S. Department of Housing and Urban Development
451 7th St. SW
Washington, DC 20410
(202) 755-5111

GLOSSARY
OF TERMS

The world of real estate uses hundreds of "insider" terms and technical terms to describe parts of the industry that are unique to it. Patient practitioners may be willing to stop along the way to define words for you, but don't count on it. You will be a more confident shopper if you become familiar enough with the terms to hold your own in the many discussions you will have to engage in. This glossary lists the most common terms you can expect to encounter. Italicized words are defined in other entries.

Abstract of title Condensed history of *title* to property that includes the chain of ownership and a record of all *liens,* taxes or other *encumbrances* that may affect the title.

Acceleration clause Clause in a loan agreement that gives the lender the right to demand full payment on the remaining balance of the loan if certain events occur.

Addendum Attachment to a *contract.* It is often placed on an additional sheet of paper and referred to in the main contract document. Also called a rider.

Adjustable-rate mortgage (ARM) Mortgage whose interest rate fluctuates depending on a previously agreed-upon *index.*

Agent Someone who acts on behalf of another. In real estate, agents work for buyers and sellers, called *principals (1).*

Amortization System of loan repayment whereby *principal (2)* and *interest* are calculated for the life of the loan and the interest is based on the declining balance of the principal.

Appraisal   Assessment of the value of a piece of property as of a specified date, usually made by an expert in the field.

Assessed value   Value of a piece of property as set by the government for taxation.

Assumable mortgage   Loan that can be taken over by another party, such as a future buyer. One benefit of the arrangement is that, if the interest rate of the original loan is lower than the current prevailing rates, its transfer to the new buyer results in substantial savings.

Attachment   Method by which real or *personal property* is legally taken by a creditor and held pending the outcome of a lawsuit over a debt.

Balloon mortgage   *Mortgage* that is paid back in a few low payments and one very large payment at the end of the mortgage.

Binder   "Agreement to agree" signed by buyer and seller. It states the agreed-upon price for the property and forbids the seller to contract with other buyers.

Breach of contract   Reason for suing based on failure to live up to a legally binding promise, such as a real estate *contract.*

Bylaws   Governing document of a *condominium* or *cooperative* association.

Cap   Limit on interest rates or individual payment rates for loans.

Certificate of title   Document stating that the seller has a good and *marketable title.*

Chain of title   List of owners of a piece of property. It is checked each time a home is sold to ensure that full and total ownership was transferred at each sale.

Closing   Formal meeting of all those involved in the sale of real estate to exchange documents and money and execute the final deal.

Closing agent   Person who oversees the *closing* process. This may be one already involved in the transaction, such as a title insurance representative or one of the *agents* of the buyer or seller.

Collateral   Something of value provisionally given to the lender during the life of the loan. In the event of *default*, it can be seized and sold by the lender.

Commission   Fixed percentage of a price paid to others (e.g., a *real estate* or *mortgage broker*) for an agreed-upon service.

Commitment fee   One-time fee paid by a buyer to a lender to bind the lender to the loan. It usually equals 1%, or one *point,* of the loan amount.

Common area   That part of a *condominium* or *cooperative* that is shared and used by all residents and paid for from the general fees charged to all unit owners.

Condominium   Form of property ownership in which individuals own and control their own units and share the costs of the *common areas* with other unit owners.

Conforming mortgage   Mortgage that conforms to the standards set by the secondary mortgage market, those who buy loans from primary lenders.

Contingency   Provision in a real estate *contract* that makes a buyer's offer to purchase dependent on certain events or terms.

Contract   Binding agreement between two parties who have willingly exchanged something of value, called the consideration.

Conversion   Change of type of ownership of a property to a *condominium* or *cooperative*. This change is regulated by state or local law.

Cooperative   Form of pooled property ownership in which individuals own shares of stock in a cooperative association that owns the property; shareholders are given control over their individual units.

Cosigner   One who adds his or her signature to the loan of another and thereby assumes equal responsibility for payments on that loan.

Convey   To transfer property to another.

Credit bureau   Company that maintains records of consumers' credit history for potential creditors, who pay a fee for the report.

Deed   Formal representation of ownership of a piece of property.

Deed of trust   Loan made by a lender to a buyer for the purchase of real estate.

Default   Declaration by a lender that a borrower has failed to make scheduled payments on a loan, thereby enabling the lender to seize the property or other *collateral.*

Disclosure   Affirmative statement made to ensure certain information is communicated. Lenders and brokers are required to make disclosures to their clients.

Discount points   See *Points.*

Down payment   That part of the purchase price given to a seller at the time of *closing*, over and above the amount of the loan.

Due on sale clause   Clause in a *mortgage* agreement that requires the balance to be paid in full when the property or *collateral* is sold. This clause forbids the *mortgage* from being *assumable.*

Earnest money   Also called a deposit. Money given by the buyer to the seller at the signing of the *binder* to demonstrate good faith.

Easement   Right to have a limited, specified use of someone else's property.

Eminent domain   Government's power to take private property for public use simply by paying for it.

Encumbrance   Anything that affects *title* to property, such as a *lien* or *mortgage.*

Equitable title   Form of ownership that is transferred when the papers are signed but actual possession is delayed. With it, responsibility for the property passes to the new owner.

Equity   Value of that part of real estate an owner has actually paid for and owns. Often it refers to that part of the total *mortgage* payments already paid, excluding *interest,* taxes and other fees plus the down payment and any appreciated value.

Escrow   Money placed in a separate account to be used in previously agreed-to circumstances and released when certain conditions are met. Escrow money is often used to pay tax and insurance bills on property during the life of a *mortgage.*

Exclusive listing contract   Agreement between a seller and *real estate broker* giving the broker the sole right to locate buyers for the listed property.

Fee simple   Absolute and total ownership of a piece of property.

Fee tail   Ownership of a piece of property that can be transferred only to one's familial heirs. A centuries-old form of ownership now not permitted in many states.

FHA loan   Loan backed by the government and made to individuals who meet certain criteria.

Fiduciary duty   Legal obligation to represent the best interests of another.

Fixture   Any object firmly attached to a piece of real estate that cannot easily be removed. Fixtures are transferred with property unless otherwise specified.

Fixed-rate mortgage   *Mortgage* for which the rate of *interest* remains the same for the life of the mortgage.

Foreclosure   Process by which property offered as security for a loan is sold to pay off the debt if the borrower is unable to pay.

GI loan   See *VA loan.*

Gift letter   Statement required by a lender of loan applicants who are receiving money from another person to make a *down payment* on a *mortgage.*

Graduated-rate mortgage *Mortgage* whose payments increase each year for a number of years and then level off.

Grace period Short period, usually ten to fifteen days after a *mortgage* payment is due, during which the borrower will be assessed no late charge or additional *interest.*

Grantee Purchaser of real estate.

Grantor Seller of real estate.

Homeowner's insurance Insurance designed to protect homeowners from losses caused by fire, theft, and so on. Some lenders require that this be purchased before they approve the loan.

Index Listing of figures or rates against which the *interest* rate is measured for *mortgages.*

Inspection Formal process of examining a piece of property and its *fixtures* to determine whether it meets a buyer's needs.

Interest Payment the lender receives for lending the money. Payment of interest creates no *equity.*

Lien Legal claim to hold or sell property as security for a debt.

Life estate Ownership in a piece of property for one's lifetime only. The holder of a life estate has no power to leave it to anyone by will. That power remains with the person who gives the property to the holder of the life estate.

Listing contract Agreement made with a *real estate broker* by a seller giving the broker the right to locate a buyer.

Loan officer Lender's employee who coordinates all of the loan processes from initial application through *closing.*

Marketable title *Title* to property that is free from all *liens, encumbrances* and defects.

Market value Value a property would command if sold on the open market.

Mechanic's lien Legal claim by a service person to hold or sell property as security for a debt.

Mortgage Formal document a home buyer signs pledging the property as security for the payment of the loan taken out to buy it.

Mortgage banker Professional who controls the investment for certain funds and locates borrowers to use those funds.

Mortgage broker Professional who matches borrowers with *mortgage* opportunities.

Mortgage servicing company Company hired by a lender to handle all the administrative aspects of *mortgage* repayment.

Multiple listing service Arrangement by which *real estate brokers* share through a computer listing the right to sell a property that has been exclusively listed with them. The broker who had the original right to sell receives a portion of the *commission* if one of the others finds a buyer.

Negative amortization Decline in owner *equity* that occurs when the *interest* rate on a *mortgage* has risen so high that loan payments no longer are large enough to cover the interest due. This results in an increase at each payment period in the *principal (2)* that is owed.

Note Written, signed document in which a borrower acknowledges a debt and promises payment.

Open listing Arrangement by which a *real estate broker* or *agent* has a nonexclusive right to sell a property. Open listings may be given to several brokers or agents. Only the one that sells the home is entitled to a *commission.*

Origination fee One-time charge by a lender for processing the loan papers. It usually amounts to 1% of total loan. It is paid at closing as a part of the *points.*

Personal property All property other than land and *fixtures.*

Points Fee a lender collects for making a loan, paid by the buyer, seller, or both. It includes both loan *origination* and *commitment fees.* Each point equals 1% of the loan amount.

Prepayment penalty Charge that penalizes a borrower who pays off a loan earlier than required by the terms of the loan.

Prime rate *Interest* banks charge their best customers.

Principal (1) Person for whom an *agent* acts. (2) That part of every *mortgage* payment that pays the cost of the home, excluding *interest* and fees. Payment of this builds *equity.*

Private mortgage insurance Insurance required by some lenders, especially when the *down payment* is low. It ensures against loss if the borrower is unable to pay.

Probate Legal process of proving a will and making the distribution of a deceased person's assets as described in the will.

Prorate To allocate respective shares of an obligation among parties or over time.

Quitclaim deed *Deed* that transfers to another the ownership one has in a property, even if that ownership is none or encumbered. Usually used to transfer property between family members.

Real estate broker Individual licensed to engage in the business of providing ready, willing and qualified buyers for sellers of property, a service for which a *commission* is paid by the seller.

A "Realtor" is a real estate broker who belongs to the National Association of Realtors. (Also see *Mortgage broker.*)

Real property   Land and all that is affixed to it.

Redlining   Discrimination against members of minority groups by refusing to make loans for home purchases in neighborhoods or communities populated by members of those groups. It is forbidden by federal law.

Refinancing   Process of paying back one loan with the proceeds of a new one. This is often done to get a better *interest* rate and usually involves payment of *closing* costs.

Restrictive covenant   "House rule" about what residents of a given area may or may not do with their property.

Rider   See *Addendum.*

Right of survivorship   Right to inherit all property held as a co-owner.

Second mortgage   New *mortgage* based on the *equity* in an existing mortgage.

Settlement   Process by which all documents are signed and placed in order and all participants in a real estate purchase are required to keep their respective promises. Also called the *closing.*

Steering   Discriminatory act of leading minority-group members away from neighborhoods not populated by members of that group. It is forbidden by federal law.

Survey   Detailed measurement map of a property, made by a licensed surveyor. Lenders often require a survey as a condition for making a loan.

Title   Official representation of ownership that is transferred when a home is sold. Title can be "held" in the name of one or more persons.

Title search   Review of the *chain of title* by a professional to discover whether any defects, *liens* or *encumbrances* exist.

Title insurance   Insurance against damages should any claims later be found in the *title.* This is paid for by the buyer. Lenders often require that additional coverage also be purchased for them.

Transfer tax   State or local tax to be paid whenever property is transferred from one owner to another. Local custom determines who pays this tax.

Truth in lending   Federal law that requires certain *disclosures* to be made to all those who apply for a loan.

Variable-rate mortgage   See *Adjustable-rate mortgage.*

Variance   Approved exception to *zoning* laws and regulations.

VA loan   Government-backed loan available to individuals who have served in active duty in the military.

Walk-through   Final cursory *inspection* of a piece of property a buyer is about to purchase. Often done the day before *closing* and not by a professional.

Warranty   Guarantee by the seller that the condition of what is being transferred is exactly as described.

Zoning   Land-designation system that sets aside certain areas for certain uses. It usually permits *variances* in areas where a requested type of development is not permitted.

BIBLIOGRAPHY

All America's Real Estate Book, by Carolyn Janik and Ruth Rejnis. Penguin Group, 40 W. 23rd St., New York, NY 10010. 1985. $14.95. Exhaustive source of information on all aspects of buying, selling, renting and moving.

Barron's Real Estate Handbook, by Jack C. Harris and Jack Friedman. Barron's Educational Series, 250 Wireless Blvd., Hauppauge, NY 11788. 1988. $19.95.
Glossary of real estate and financial terms with chapters on buying, selling and careers in real estate. Extensive bibliography.

The Common-Sense Guide to Successful Real Estate Negotiation, by Peter G. Miller and Douglas M. Bregman. Harper and Row Publishers, 10 E. 53rd St., New York, NY 10022. 1987. $16.95.
Strategies for buying and selling house without an agent. Information you need easy to find with small sections and index. Sample contracts and forms throughout.

The Common-Sense Mortgage—How to Cut the Cost of Home Ownership by $100,000 or More, by Peter G. Miller. Harper and Row Publishers, 10 E. 53rd St., New York, NY 10022. 1987. $7.95.
Well-reviewed do-it-yourself book on mortgages and finances. Includes extensive index and list of relevant questions to ask.

The Complete Book of Homebuying, by Michael Sumichrast and Ronald C. Shafer. Bantam Books, 666 5th Ave., New York, NY 10103. 1987. $4.95.
Pros and cons of buying new versus older homes, doing home improvements and selling property on your own. Financing and tax information.

The Complete Guide to Real Estate Loans, by Andrew James McLean. Contemporary Books, 180 N. Michigan Ave, Chicago, IL 60601. 1983. $6.95.

Covers most major topics, but in a rather cursory manner. Large print and many charts make it easy to read, but there is not much information in this 116-page book.

The Complete Homebuyers Kit, by Edith Lank. Longman Financial Service, 520 N. Dearborn St., Chicago, IL 60610-4975. 1989. $14.95. Thorough book on all aspects of home buying including tips on choosing agent, financing purchase, comparing properties and negotiating contract. Includes mortgage rate charts.

The Complete Homesellers Kit, by Edith Lank. Longman Financial Service, 520 N. Dearborn St., Chicago, IL 60610-4975. 1988. $14.95. Useful comparisons on whether you should sell on your own or with an agent. Includes tips on negotiating sales contracts, fixing up homes and taxes. Glossary.

The Complete House Inspection Book, by Don Frederickson. Fawcett Columbine, Ballantine Books, 201 E. 50th St., New York, NY 10022. 1988. $9.95. Thorough evaluation from author, former plumber, electrician, builder and inspector, of all parts and possible defects in a home. Encourages making your own evaluations.

The Deeds Book: How to Transfer Title to California Real Estate, by Mary Randolph. Nolo Press, 950 Parker St., Berkeley, CA 94710. 1987. $15.95. Step-by-step guide to changing property title in California. Includes tear-out forms.

The Field Guide to Home Buying in America, by Stephen Pollan, Mark Levine, and Michael Pollan. Simon and Schuster, 1230 Avenue of the Americas, New York, NY 10020. 1988. $8.95. Authors cover every possible question from thinking about buying to moving in.

First Home Buying Guide, by H. L. Kibbey. Panoply Press, Inc., P.O. Box 1885, Lake Oswego, OR 97035. 1988. $8.95. Useful guide for first-time home buyers on how to find a home, work with agent, get loan approved and close deal.

For Sale By Owner: All the Contracts and Instructions Necessary to Sell Your Own California House, by George Devine. Nolo Press, 950 Parker St., Berkeley, CA 94710. 1987. $24.95. Home-selling tips for California residents. Includes glossary and tear-out contracts and forms.

Home Buyers: Lambs to Slaughter, by Sloan Bashinsky, Menasha Ridge Press, Route 3, Box 450 HB, Hillsborough, NC 27278. 1984. $12.95. Short, complete look at real estate "game." Describes your allies and opponents, contains table of how to figure monthly mortgage costs.

How to Buy a Home While You Can Still Afford To, by Michael C. Murphy. Sterling Publications Co., 387 Park Ave. South, New York, NY 10016. 1989. $7.95.

Tips on finding mortgage, using short-term loans, computing tax advantages. Includes worksheets.

How to Buy a House, Condo or Co-op, by Michael C. Thomsett. Consumer Report Books, 51 E. 42nd St., New York, NY 10017. 1987. $12.00.

For first- and second-time home buyers; information includes locating property, negotiating prices, closing deals. Index and glossary.

How to Buy a House When You Are Cash Poor, by Vanessa A. Bush. Contemporary Books, 180 N. Michigan Ave., Chicago, IL 60601. 1986. $4.95.

Evaluates various mortgage systems and ways of financing home purchase. Lists areas of house essential to inspect before buying.

How to Buy Your Home in 90 Days, by Marc Stephen Garrison. Doubleday Publishing Co., 666 5th Ave., New York, NY 10103. 1989. $12.95.

Tips for novice on financing, dealing with brokers, negotiating best possible price and closing deal. Includes amortization schedules and glossary.

How to Sell Your House Without a Broker, by Harley Bjelland. Cornerstone Library, 1230 Avenue of the Americas, New York, NY 10020. 1979. $3.95.

Fairly complete synopsis of what is involved in a sale including cleaning house, writing advertisements, financing and moving.

Making Mortgages Work for You, by Robert Irwin. McGraw-Hill Book Co., 1221 Avenue of the Americas, New York, NY 10020. 1987. $12.95.

Major financing options in well-organized and easy-to-read fashion. Lengthy appendix helps determine how much money to spend under variety of interest rates.

The New Real Estate Game, by Hollis Norton. Contemporary Books, 180 N. Michigan Ave., Chicago, IL 60601. 1987. $17.95.

Tips on how to get financing, buy and sell properties, renovate and juggle tax laws to your financial advantage.

Nothing Down, by Robert G. Allen. Simon and Schuster, 1230 Avenue of the Americas, New York, NY 10020. 1984. $19.95.

For the real estate investor, offers creative financing tips if you have little or no money to put down and information on how to manage properties.

101 Easy Ways to Make Your Home Sell Faster, by Barbara Jane Hall. Ballantine Books, 201 E. 50th St., New York, NY 10022. 1985. $4.95.

How to present your home in best possible light to prospective buyers, including interior decoration.

Power Real Estate Negotiations, by William H. Pivar and Richard W. Post. Longman Financial Services, 520 N. Dearborn St., Chicago, IL 60610-4975. 1990. $19.95.

Useful resource for investors and real estate professionals. Covers general negotiating strategies for every aspect of buying and selling property.

Selling Your Home Sweet Home: A Practical Survival Guide for Selling Your Home, by Sloan Bashinsky. Monarch Press, 1230 Avenue of the Americas, New York, NY 10020. 1985. $12.95.

With innovative ways to get the highest price for your house, this book will help you deal with professionals, prepare your house, set a price, finance, negotiate and more. Ethical codes, regulatory agencies and a sample grievance complaint form included.

The Single Person's Home-Buying Handbook, by Kristelle L. Petersen. Hawthorn/Dutton, 2 Park Ave., New York, NY 10016. 1980. $6.95 (Out of print.)

Useful information for single people, emphasizing legal concerns and protections still useful but should be supplemented with more recent information on financing and tax considerations. Index and glossary.

Sonny Bloch's Inside Real Estate, by H. I. Sonny Bloch and Grace Lichtenstein. Weidenfield and Nicolson, 10 East 53rd St., New York, NY 10022. 1987. $18.95.

Role of both seller and buyer in each side of real estate transaction. Glossary and amortization tables included.

Sonny Bloch's 171 Ways to Make Money in Real Estate, by Sonny Bloch and Grace Lichtenstein. Prentice-Hall Press, 15 Columbus Circle, New York, NY 10023. 1989. $19.95.

Step-by-step instructions through every phase of investment process. Includes sample contracts, rental and purchase agreements, financial portfolios and more.

Top Dollar for Your Property, by James E. A. Lumley. John Wiley and Sons, 605 Third Ave., New York, NY 10158-0012. 1988. $12.95. Good guide to all aspects of selling your home. Well-organized and easy to read.

Webster's New World Illustrated Encyclopedic Dictionary of Real Estate, by Jerome S. Gross. Simon and Schuster, One Gulf and Western Plaza, New York, NY 10023. 1987. $12.95.
Includes complete dictionary of terms, portfolio of forms, list of organizations, amortization schedule, and National Association of Realtors Code of Ethics.

About the Author

George Milko is the director of education for HALT, specializing in alternatives to lawsuits, torts and liability, personal injury and mass disaster litigation. He is editor of *Alternative Compensation Strategies: Creating No Lawsuit Options To the Tort System,* and coauthor of *After the Crash: An Information Kit For Victims of Airline Disasters* and *Everyday Contracts.* He received his law degree from the National Law Center at George Washington University and is a member of the District of Columbia Bar.